Ancient INDIAN Artifacts

VOLUME 2

Collecting Flint Weapons & Tools

IDENTIFICATION & VALUES

Jim Bennett

COLLECTOR BOOKS
A Division of Schroeder Publishing Co., Inc.

Cover design by Terri Hunter
Book design by Beth Ray

COLLECTOR BOOKS
P.O. Box 3009
Paducah, Kentucky 42002-3009

www.collectorbooks.com

Copyright © 2010 Jim Bennett

All rights reserved. No part of this book may be reproduced, stored in any retrieval system, or transmitted in any form, or by any means including but not limited to electronic, mechanical, photocopy, recording, or otherwise, without the written consent of the author and publisher.

The current values in this book should be used only as a guide. They are not intended to set prices, which vary from one section of the country to another. Auction prices as well as dealer prices vary greatly and are affected by condition as well as demand. Neither the author nor the publisher assumes responsibility for any losses that might be incured as a result of consulting this guide.

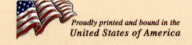

Proudly printed and bound in the United States of America

CONTENTS

- Dedication 4
- Acknowledgments 4
- Author's Note 4
- Introduction 5
- Common Flint Artifact Traits 7
- Is It an Artifact? If so, What Is It? 17
- Identifying Point Types, Time Periods, and Locations of Finds 19
- Projectile Points 20
  - Lances 20
  - Dart Points 28
  - Arrowpoints 46
  - Birdpoints 57
  - Gempoints 61
- Knives and Blades 64
  - Hand Knives and Blades 64
- Uniface and Biface Flake Knives 72
- Hafted Knives 75
- Tang Knives 155
- Bi-pointed Knives 158
- Crescent Knives 161
- Square Knives 163
- Four Bevel Knives 165
  - Exhausted Knives 165
- Chopping Tools 167
  - Flint Axes 167
  - Flint Celts 170
  - Flint Adzes 178
- Farming and Digging Tools 179
  - Hoes and Spades 180
  - Diggers 185
- Perforating Tools 186
  - Drills 186
  - Awls, Reamers, and Perforators 197
- Woodworking Tools 198
  - Flint Chisels 198
  - Spokeshaves and Shaft Scrapers 201
- Scrapers 206
  - Hafted Scrapers 207
  - Thumb Scrapers 209
  - Hand Scrapers 210
  - Gouge Tip Blunts 211
- Miscellaneous Flint Artifacts 212
  - Eccentrics 212
  - Cores 213
  - Lancets and Bladlets 215
  - Flint Saws 216
  - Multi-purpose Tools 216
  - Flint Hammerstones and Knapping Stones 218
  - Caches and Cache Blades 219
- Authenticity Issues 228
- Show and Tell 229

DEDICATION

To my fiance, Angela, for making sure I was up early before work each morning to write this book, and for all of the cups of coffee brought to my desk so I could wake enough to write coherently — but mostly for understanding and appreciating my love for artifacts and writing.

ACKNOWLEDGMENTS

It would be impossible to complete books such as this without the assistance of fellow collectors submitting pictures, scans, stories, and information, and allowing their collections to be photographed. For this book, over 50 individuals contributed photographs. To each one of you I am eternally grateful for your assistance. I would list out all of the names here were not for the fear that I may neglect someone.

A special thanks goes to my good friends David Bogle and Matt Rowe at the Museum of Native American Artifacts and to Keith Ray and Rob Dills of Ohio Valley Artifacts for once again assisting with last minute photography and point type identification.

AUTHOR'S NOTE

While current value information is included on many of the artifacts in this book, some artifact values are represented as "personal find" or "value unlisted." The reason for this is that personally finding a nice artifact adds a level of appreciation for the artifact found that often cannot be expressed by monetary means. Most collectors do not sell their personal finds and do not like to see values placed on their personally found relics. Out of respect they are listed here simply as "personal find." For other various reasons some collectors only allow their artifacts to be pictured without value information. As collecting is about appreciation of the artifacts and what they represent, some artifact photographs have been used with their value simply stated as "unlisted."

INTRODUCTION

Slowly walking along with my head bent down and my eyes scanning left and right, a little spot of black coloration caught my attention about three feet to my right, causing me to quickly stop. Beetle? Piece of plastic? Rotting leaf? Bird dropping? Or — more hopefully — Coshocton flint. Most of the artifacts I had found in this area over the years were made of the Coshocton variety, so anything black or gray was quick to prompt my attention. I reached over with my walking stick and prodded it. Yep, definitely hard. I took a couple steps closer and bent down. As the item came into clearer view, what was an obscure black spot from three or four feet away grew as I drew closer, leaving no doubt it was flint, and the visibly flaked surface left no doubt it was worked — I had found an artifact. I smiled, becoming hopeful as to what exactly I had come across. Leaning on my walking stick and kneeling down, I studied the small half-inch section that was exposed. I didn't see a tip or a base, just a small area of flaked flint that was definitely part of something larger that remained mostly under the washed dirt, but what? And just how large? It is at this point that a collector's mind tends to have a bit of fun with him. Knowing that the odds are it is most likely just part of a broken point, scraper, or a section of a knife that has been busted up by a 150 years of farming, it is still hard not to hope for that elusive Clovis or Dovetail. I slowly reached for it, wiggled it free and began gently rubbing the dirt from it with my thumb and fore-finger as a nicely made little scraper began to take shape. How many different scrapers had I found in this field over the last two decades I pondered. Twenty? Thirty? I couldn't remember exactly, but it was definitely more than a few. I just smiled, scraper in hand, reminding myself that any find is a good find. Maybe tomorrow will be the day I come across that Dove or Clovis. After 20 years of tomorrows in this field, I had to be getting closer to the tomorrow that would pay off.

This 1¼" corner notch hafted scraper is made from petrified wood. While it is not one that I found, when my friend and fellow collector John Selmer sent this photograph to me, it brought back the fond memories recorded in this story. Found in New Mexico. Collection of John Selmer.

Leaning on my walking stick I stood up, chuckling to myself as I did so. Twenty years ago I carried a walking stick simply to flip out rocks that were perspective artifacts and to poke at triangle shaped leaves I thought to myself. How many times have I poked at stones that might have been grooved, or flat pieces of slate that sure looked like they were something until they were flipped out. Now, I carry a walking stick to ease my aching knees when I kneel down or stand up. I might only be 45 I thought, but my knees have got to be in their 80s. I continued to smile and shook my head at myself as I wondered if electric powered wheelchairs could be retro-fitted with all-terrain tires. I would worry about that down the road, for now the walking stick still does the trick.

I stood there for a few minutes taking a little break and fondling the scraper that soon would find a new home in one of my tool frames while taking in the view of the surrounding area and letting my mind wander. The 10 acre field I was in was generally flat, falling off on one side down to a creek and gently rising on the other side to another field that was off limits to relic hunting for the rest of the summer due to the fast growth of the soy beans, turning the beautifully tilled surface of that field into a lush green carpet of leaves. I thought how glad I was that this year was a "corn year" in the farmer's rotation for the field I was in, giving me ample time to hunt the surface and recover the scattered evidence of cultures long past before the plow took its further toll on them. Over the last 10 years this little field had proved to be one of my favorite spots to spend a few hours after work on a warm spring day before the crops took over and the ground was lost from view.

On more than one occasion while traversing this little plot of land I would pause and look around, trying to imagine what it looked like two, four, or even eight thousand years ago. How tall were the trees back then I wondered? Was there a clearing here or was it forest? How much water flowed through the creek in those days? Why was this exact spot chosen for a camp area rather than any other spot along this creek? I stood there, gazing around and thinking about all the various items I had picked up in this field over the last two decades. Hafted scrapers and dart points, Archaic knives and Mississippian triangle points, and the occasional field celt or broken pendant. While this little spot of earth was only one of thousands of such little camp areas used in ancient times here in Ohio, the evidence collected from the surface of the furrowed rows left no doubt that I was simply one of many who stood in this spot and gazed at the beauty of the surrounding countryside.

INTRODUCTION

I have often written that the true lure of collecting artifacts goes so much deeper than the mere accumulation of the relics themselves. It's the moments like the one mentioned here that keep collectors collecting. It's not just about buying 6" Cumberlands or a Mueser knobbed banner or the current market value of Clovis points — although we all appreciate those immensely, it's the ability to look back in time and ponder when holding a thumb scraper, drill, or used-up knife about those who crafted and used them long ago. It's about standing in the middle of a field in 2010 and picturing those who stood there in 2010 BC using the very items that lay upon the surface.

In the first book of this series, we took a look at the basic artifact groups that make up the hobby of collecting ancient Indian artifacts. In this book, we will be focusing on those items that were made from flint. Keeping in mind that the term "flint artifacts" is a generic collector's term for flaked artifacts, and much of the material that was flaked in ancient times was not actually flint, but rather other various types of material that were dense enough to allow for manufacture by conchodial fracture which resulted in the removal of flakes. Throughout this book we will use the term flint in this generic sense when speaking of flaked artifacts. You will find examples of artifacts made not only from true flint, but also from the numerous types of chert, agates, obsidian, petrified woods, agatized coral, and other materials that were naturally available to ancient man.

The actual intended use of flaked items in ancient times is very broad, as some were used as projectile points, while other were more utilitarian tools used for daily tasks such as chopping, scraping hides, cutting leather, and digging. What binds these items together into a collecting group is not a similarity in their ancient use, but rather the similarity in the material used in their manufacture, and the methods used to shape that material into usable tools and weapons.

COMMON FLINT ARTIFACT TRAITS

When discussing flint artifacts, collectors tend to hear certain terms used to describe specific attributes a relic may exhibit. For the experienced collector, these terms may be second nature, but for those newer to the hobby they can cause some confusion, so I wanted to include a few explanations of some the terms used throughout this book.

Commonly used flint artifact terms:

- bifacial flaking
- unifacial flaking
- resharpening
- secondary flaking
- edge serration
- basal thinning
- basal fluting
- basal and stem grinding
- preforms and blanks
- stacks/haystacks
- use polish and use wear
- fire damage
- impact fractures
- fractured base points and snapped base points
- heat treating

Bifacial Flaking
Bifacial flaking simply means that flakes were taken off both sides of a relic to reduce or re-sharpen it. In the case of manufacture, the raw material was reduced in size by taking flakes from both of the face sides of the item, leaving flake scars visible on all, or at least most, of the relic's surface. In the case of utilitarian flake knives and tools with simply a cutting edge which were made from a section of flint removed from the spall, bifacial flaking can be identified by the removal of pressure flakes from both sides along the edges to create the cutting edge.

Unifacial Flaking
In the case of unifacial flaking, the material was removed by flaking only one side of the item. With unifacial resharpening, the edge of a knife or point requiring resharpening or repair would have flakes removed from only one side of the blade edge.

Resharpening
When the edge of a knife or tool became dull from use, the ancient user would re-sharpen it by removing another row of flakes along the blade edges. Sometimes this was done bifacially, while other times this would be done unifacially. In the case of unifacial resharpening, beveling of the blade edges could occur after multiple resharpenings.

Secondary Flaking
Secondary flaking is just another term used for the pressure-flaked areas of an item. Since percussion flaking came first in the manufacture process, pressure flaking is occasionally referred to as secondary flaking.

Edge Serrations
Just as we use serrated knives today for cutting, so did ancient man. Serrations were often placed intentionally along blade edges of a knife to assist with cutting. Serrations can also occasionally be seen along the edges of some projectile points.

Ohio Thebes E-notch bevel knife with serrated edges. Found in Ohio. Collection of Rob Dills. $100.00 – 150.00.

Serrated Ohio knife from the Keith Ray collection. $60.00 – 80.00.

Common Flint Artifact Traits

2⅛" bifurcated base knife with serrated edges. Found in Ohio. Collection of Keith Ray. $50.00 – 60.00.

Excellent example of "micro-serrations" along the edge of this nice Indiana Thebes "E" notch. Collection of Keith Ray. $800.00 – 1,000.00.

Basal Thinning

When hafting a knife or a projectile point to a shaft or handle, the base would be inserted into a slot cut into the receiving end and then glued and tied in place. In order to minimize the width of the slot necessary, the base of the point or knife would often be thinned on one or both sides by removing flakes from the base of the point upward toward the middle of the item. This is known as basal thinning.

Transitional Paleo stemmed point found in Ohio that exhibits basal thinning. Collection of Keith Ray. $80.00 – 100.00.

Basal Fluting

While basal fluting and basal thinning were both done for the same purpose, to reduce the thickness of the base of an item being hafted, different techniques were used to achieve these similar results. The term basal thinning is generally applied to items with multiple flakes removed from the base. Basal fluting is a totally different technique that allowed the crafter to remove one large flake from the base traveling upward toward the tip leaving a channel on one or both sides of the point, lance, or knife. Fluting was limited to the Paleo period. Why ancient man strayed from this technique in ancient times is unknown, although several theories exist. The most plausible theory to me is that with the extinction of the mega-fauna mammals such as the wooly mammoth, thrusting spears and dart points no longer needed to be as thin to penetrate deep enough into an animal to strike a vital organ. As the fluting step is applied toward the end of the manufacture process and could easily result in breakage of the item being crafted, the technique was left behind.

Very nice 1⅛" long fluted Folsom point found by Carlos Black in Kaufman Co., Texas, in 2006. Unlisted.

Basal and Stem Grinding

The freshly flaked edge of a flint item is extremely sharp. When tying a point or knife to a shaft or handle the material used to tie with could easily be cut when it was pulled tight to secure the item being hafted. Grinding or sanding down the base and many times the lower edges of the item would help keep this from happening. Different styles of points and knives in different time periods are known to have basal grinding present. Most all Paleo points and knives were well ground, as were various styles that were created thoughout all of the following time periods.

Ohio Dovetail from the Keith Ray collection that exhibits nice basal grinding. Note the rounded look to the edge of the base.

Big Sandy point from Ohio with a nicely ground base. Collection of Keith Ray.

Preforms and Blanks

Walking for several days back to his camp or village from a visit to a quarry site with a rock that might not even flake well was not something ancient man wanted to do. So, he would go to the flint source, quarry some flint, and knap the flint into performs which are also called blanks or quarry blanks. This would allow the knapper to bring back only the pieces of flint that he felt confident would be able to be completed, and maximize the amount of usable flint he could carry. When I visited the Flint Ridge quarry site in Licking Co., Ohio, I was amazed at the amount of broken and discarded blanks scattered about the area. Blanks that were started, but either broke due to impurities in the material or blanks that the knapper saw too many problematical areas in and tossed aside.

Once these blanks were back at the camp or village, the knapper could then select at his convenience the preform that would best suit his needs for whatever item he was preparing to craft. Often caches, or quantities of blanks, are found at or near areas of ancient occupation. Since blanks are generally considered unfinished and are fairly crude in style and flaking, they hold a very minimal value.

Common Flint Artifact Traits

4½" to 4¾" preforms made from Burlington. Found in Webster Co., Missouri. Collection of Stephen Burks. $5.00 – 10.00.

2⅞" Paleo preform made from Knife River flint. Found in Morton Co., North Dakota. $10.00 – 15.00.

Set of blanks from Ashland Co., Ohio, from the author's collection. $1.00 – 3.00.

5" Dovetail preform made of Coshocton flint. Found in Coshocton Co., Ohio. Collection of John Lutz. $60.00 – 80.00.

Set of blanks from Ashland Co., Ohio, from the author's collection. $1.00 – 3.00.

Stacks/Haystacks

I once wrote that the art of flint knapping is similar to any other art form in that not all art is good art. Sometimes, it is the lack of skill of the crafter; other times it is no fault at all of the knapper, but rather the lack of quality of the material he was working with. Most any flint knapper will tell you that each piece of flint is different from the next as to how it is going to react during the manufacture process. Some flint has few impurities or potential problem areas, while other sections of flint can be fraught with problematical areas. Depending on the quality of the material used and the impurities within it, certain areas can be troublesome to flake. A commonly seen result from such areas are stacks or haystacks. These are areas on the surface of the relic that just didn't want to flake nicely, and result in high spots that either couldn't be or wouldn't be easily removed, leaving the item thicker than normal in a given area. Such areas are caused when a flake is removed, but terminates early without traveling nicely across the surface of the flint. Often times, the knapper will make several attempts at removing these high spots only to accentuate the problem area. As flint artifacts are judged by their uniformity in flaking and lenticular thinness, these high spots are seen as negatively affecting an artifacts optimum value.

The ancient crafter tried hard to get the flaking right on the upper portion of this Florida dart point, but as seen by the large stacks that remain, it was to no avail.

Use Polish and Use Wear

The terms "use wear" and "use polish" are used nearly synonymously when describing areas on an artifact that have been worn down from use. The worn area generally has a polished look to the surface of the area affected. The only difference that can be argued between the two terms is that use polish is applied more to the polished look found on the surface of the flint from repeated use, and use wear can also be used to describe areas on the relic that have actually been damaged from repeated use. An example of this would be the blade edge of a serrated knife; the term use wear can be applied when describing serrations that have broken off during use.
There are generally three types of wear that an artifact may have that results in a polishing:

1.) Wear from contact with other materials being worked.
Examples of wear caused by this type of contact would be the bit of a flint celt used to chop wood for a long period of time. The high spots on the flint near the bit can become polished from the repeated contact with the wood. Flint drills and scrapers often exhibit use wear on their tips from the repeated drilling and scraping that puts the bit areas of these tools in direct contact with the material being worked. The most extreme examples of use polish caused by contact is seen on flint hoes. Used for long periods of time to loosen dirt, the repeated contact with the ground can leave an exceptionally high polish on the bit area of the hoes.

2.) Wear from contact with the handle if it were a hafted items.
Worn areas can appear around the area of a flint artifact that was hafted to a handle. In the case of a knife, if it were loosely hafted, wear on the high spots around the middle of the base can occasionally be seen. With hoes, which for some reason were often more loosely hafted (possibly due to their size and lack of use of an adhesive), wear and occasional high polish can be seen on the top part of the hoe where it was attached to the handle. In the case of flint celts, wear can be seen on the midsection or rear poll area. With notched celts and hoes, wear polish can often be seen in the area on the surface between the notches as well on the side edges.

3.) Wear from being held directly in hand for a long period of time.

In the case of hand held tools that were used for long periods of time before being lost or discarded, occasionally you can find worn down and polished areas on the surface of the flint that was in the most direct contact with the user's hand. Often, I will take a hand tool and hold it to see how fits in hand, and then look for such areas on the surface.

Fire Damage

An interesting trait that can be seen on some flint artifacts is fire damage — also called fire pops or blow-outs. When flint gets over-heated, the moisture in the stone expands and the stone itself can come apart, usually leaving a crater-like appearance. In some cases, a single pop will be present, while in other cases, a whole area on the surface may exhibit multiple craters or pops. The presence of fire pops greatly diminishes the value of an artifact.

This Tennessee stemmed point shows an area of fire damage near the base. Note the rough looking appearance of the flint in the fire pop area.

Stemmed point showing severe fire damage.

Impact Fracture

When the tip of a flint point or knife comes in contact with a hard object that places pressure directly against the tip, it can cause an impact fracture. Examples of this would be a projectile point missing its target and coming in contact with a hard object or hitting its target and directly striking a bone. For knives, impact fractures can occur if the tip of the knife strikes a bone during butchering or strikes a rock in the ground. Impact fractures can be found on most any flint tool type. The resulting damage is an area on the tip that removes a flake or section of flint traveling from the point down toward the middle of the item.

Impact fractures can be frontal fractures, meaning the inertia traveled down one or both faces of the surface, or lateral, meaning the inertia traveled down the side or edge of the item.

Fractured Base Points and Snapped Base Points

Why some points were manufactured a specific and certain way may never be known. True fractured base points are one of those styles. On Decatur style points, as well as some other styles, the very bottom of the base was fractured from each side, and then ground over. This technique is called "burinating" or "burin fracturing," "burin flaking," or "burin faceting." A burin facet is flat in appearance and rather than traveling flat across the surface of the relic is placed along one of the relic's outer edges. On fractured base points there usually is a small step in the center of the base where the two burin fractures meet. This point style is one of the rarer styles to collect.

Snapped base points on the other hand are not at all the same as fractured bases. With snapped base points, the base has been broken off across the entire length of the base. Evidence of the snapped area can usually be seen traveling up the flat surface of one side of the base area. Snapped base points are not shaped using the burin fracture technique. While some type guides will list snapped base points as an intentionally made style, I have yet to see or read any evidence that this was done intentionally during the manufacturing process. My personal opinion is that snapped base points are simply damaged points or knives that were hafted and then broke during use due to too much stress to the hafting area. It is possible that a knife could have broken (snapped) at the base and then was re-hafted if enough of the base remained, but as the base of a point was intentionally created to be inserted into the receiving end of the haft to strengthen the tool — especially at the haft — intentionally removing this vital area to leave a thick and somewhat bulky base would serve no logical purpose.

Fractured base point found in Ohio. Note the fractures that were intentionally placed coming in from both sides that were then ground over. Collection of Rob Dills.

2 1/16" Decatur made from hornstone. Found in Indiana. Collection of Musée de la Neufve. Photo by Nicolas Tremblay. $150.00 – 250.00.

3 1/4" Flint Ridge fracture base point found in Muskingum Co., Ohio. Collection of Mike Diano. $800.00 – 1,000.00.

Fractured base point found in Wayne Co., Kentucky. Collection of Randall Carrier. $150.00 – 250.00.

Common Flint Artifact Traits

Snapped Base Damaged Points

Assortment of points with snapped bases that were broken during use. Found in Ashland Co., Ohio. Author's collection.

Another type of fractured base that is seen on select of flint points also utilized the burin faceting technique; however, rather than traveling across the bottom of the base, on this style it travels upward as seen on the Lake Erie bifurcate style dart points. Why this was done may never be known, but it is found on a very few select styles of bifurcated points.

Nice selection of Lake Erie bifurcate points from the collection of Keith Ray. $10.00 – 80.00.

Common Flint Artifact Traits

Heat Treated Flint

How soft or how brittle a certain type of material is has a lot to do with how easy it will be to manage once flaking has begun. At some point after the Paleo period had ended, ancient man learned that by heating the raw flint blanks before beginning the flaking process, the material would undergo a change and it would be easier to control when being shaped. The heat actually causes a molecular change resulting in a difference in the stone's hardness, making the material easier to work. One great attribute for artifact collectors is that often the heat treating process would change the color and texture of the surface of the stone, adding some wonderful colors and often a glossy look and feel. It is believed that in order not to over heat the material being treated, ancient man would place preforms in the bottom of a shallow hole and then cover them with a layer of dirt. Hot coals were then placed on top of the dirt with the heat traveling down to the blanks.

While heat treating occurred in many areas, one of best places to see examples of this technology is found in Florida. Florida artifacts made from heat-treated materials ranging from cherts to agatized coral are some of the most beautiful artifacts found in North America.

The following Florida artifacts are made from heat-treated materials.

3 3/8" Newnan found in Hillsborough Co., Florida, and made from heat-treated agatized coral. Rick Schwardt collection. Museum quality.

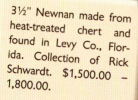

4 9/16" Newnan made from heat-treated Pinhead coral. Found in Hernando Co., Florida. Rick Schwardt collection. Museum quality.

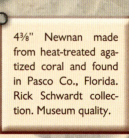

3 1/2" Newnan made from heat-treated chert and found in Levy Co., Florida. Collection of Rick Schwardt. $1,500.00 – 1,800.00.

4 3/8" Newnan made from heat-treated agatized coral and found in Pasco Co., Florida. Rick Schwardt collection. Museum quality.

Common Flint Artifact Traits

The unheated material used for the previous relics is not as glossy as the heated varieties shown above, but heated or unheated, there is no doubt the ancient craftsmanship and material used from that area makes for some truly beautiful artifacts.

This nice 3⅛" Kirk point is made from unheated coral and was found in Pasco Co., Florida. Rick Schwardt collection. $350.00 – 500.00.

2¹¹⁄₁₆" Clay point and 3³⁄₁₆" Citrus point found in Florida and made from unheated chert. Rick Schwardt collection. Values unlisted.

Pair of Florida Hernando points made from un-heated chert and measuring 2⅜". Rick Schwardt collection. Values unlisted.

Pair of Clay knives found together in Levy Co., Florida, by Rick Schwardt and made from unheated material. Personal finds.

IS IT AN ARTIFACT? IF SO, WHAT IS IT?

I get scores of emails each month from people who have found "something" in their yard, garden, or a nearby field, and they are curious if what they have found is an artifact. For seasoned collectors, noticing the signs of manufacture is second nature when looking at pieces of flint. For people not familiar with flint artifacts, everything can easily appear to be an artifact. The more material a new collector handles, the easier it is to identify if something has actually been worked by ancient man. Even after years of collecting, I still drag pieces out of the field to clean up — only to contribute them later to the flowerbed in front of the house as either "close but no cigar" or too badly broken to really display. I think it is common practice for collectors to drag items out of the field, and since our love for artifacts and history will not allow us to discard anything collected, many collectors tend to decorate areas around the outside of the house with leftovers. One evening during the AACA National Artifact Expo weekend which is held outside of Cincinnati, Ohio, each July, a friend and I were invited to view the collection of Charlie Wagers, a well known Ohio collector who has assembled a truly world class collection. I had been to his house once before years earlier shooting photos, and I was going from memory on how to find his house. We pulled into the driveway of a house I was fairly certain was his, and we rang the doorbell. While standing there waiting, my friend asked if I was sure we had the right house. At that point we both glanced around at the artifacts and debitage scattered in the flowerbeds and my friend said "well, if it's not Charlie's house, at least we know this person collects relics."

At first I wasn't sure this was a relic as one side was quite thick and flat, but once I handled it and saw the nice bifacially flaked edge, there was no doubt this was an ancient knife. Made from petrified wood, found in Colorado. Author's collection.

Determining if an item is an artifact or not simply comes down to determining if a piece of natural material was altered intentionally by man for a specific purpose. Ancient man was limited in technology to only using one of several manufacturing techniques to turn stone into tools and weapons. For tools made from hardstone, the surface was pecked with a hammerstone and then polished over. With flint artifacts, alterations to the natural shape of the stone were made by removing flakes using percussion and pressure flaking. Since not all types of stone will flake nicely, ancient man sought out those material types that would, such as flint, chert, and other dense materials that had a grain pattern conducive to conchoidial fracture. Breaking any rock is not a hard thing to do. You hit it hard enough, it is going to break. But can that break be controlled enough to create a specific shape? This is is the reason ancient man only used specific types of materials for manufacture. Flint, chert, obsidian, and other such materials that were used could be controlled by the amount of stress applied to their surface. Flaking is simply applying the correct amount of pressure at the proper location to remove a desired amount of material to create a specific pattern or form. Conchoidial fracture means that when this stress was placed correctly it would result in a curved fracture pattern.

As discussed in the first book in this series, percussion flaking would be used to remove larger sections of material, followed by pressure flaking to help finalize the shape and sharpen the edges. Which brings us to the first question at hand — is it an artifact? If the flint does not show signs of percussion or pressure flaking, then it lacks the evidence that it is an actual artifact. Many times flint will have

Small pieces of flint debitage leftover from the manufacturing process. Debitage pieces do not exhibit any secondary flaking along their edges.

signs of percussion flaking, but will totally lack any style or shape that identifies it as a usable tool. Keep in mind that during the manufacture process, larger pieces of worked flint were removed from the item being made to reduce the size of the object in order to obtain the final shape and style of the end product. Hence, many pieces of removed flint known as "debitage" are simply left-overs from this process. While pieces of debitage are artifacts in one way as they are the result of work by ancient man, they are not completed items that were used for a specific task and hence are not often collected and maintain no collectible value.

Now to the second part of the question – if it is worked, then what was it? Ancient man made many tools from flint for various different tasks. Many styles are easy to recognize such as points, knives, scrapers, and spokeshaves, while others shapes and styles leave some room for speculation. Throughout this book we will look at many of the different tool types that were made from flint in prehistoric times for specific purposes. While this is not a complete encyclopedia of every tool type ever flaked in ancient times, most of the major items made from flint are covered in detail.

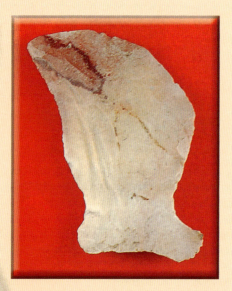
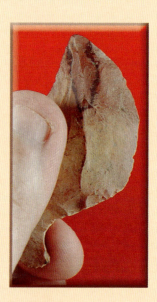

This artifact is a large flake removed from a flint spall. At first it looked like a piece of debitage, but upon closer examination small pressure flakes could be seen along one edge confirming its use as a knife or scraper. Author's collection. $10.00 – 20.00.

IDENTIFYING POINT TYPES, TIME PERIODS, AND LOCATIONS OF FINDS

One of the most amazing things to me when pondering random thoughts about artifacts is the exactness in style that was replicated thousands of times over. Once a style was found to work, for whatever reason, it would become the template for tens of thousands or more of the same design. Considering we are discussing a time when communication was limited to face to face contact, there can be no doubt that common communication existed not only between local villages, but also across vast areas when looking at the exactness of the styles that were used in large areas for long periods of time.

One of first things to look at when deciding what type a point might be, or what general time period it is from, is the base. Once the general basal style is determined, then the hunt for smaller differentiating characteristics such as lobes, incurvated and excurvated areas, and basal grinding and thinning can help to narrow down the search for the proper type name. The way the base was designed is connected directly to the manner in which the point or knife was hafted or tied to a handle, dart, or arrow shaft. With the exception of certain suspension knives such as some tang knives, most all notched artifacts were hafted in one manner or another.

Using typology books can be a very frustrating endevour. There are so many named types these days, separated by the smallest of differences, that many collectors, especially the old timers, tend to stick with the basic description of basal style when discussing what a point type is. Archiac sidenotch, stemmed lance, paleo lanceolate, etc. often is as close as many wish to go in the typology area. Combine the fact that many times the same basic style point has multiple names depending on what part of the country it is from or who wrote the typology book, and the confusion can be overwhelming for new collectors as well as too frustrating for seasoned collectors to care what the exact type is. When standing at the table of a long-time collector at a show recently, I was pondering whether a specific point on his table was a smaller MacCorkle or a larger nicely made Kanawha. He smiled at me and said to him it was "a bifurcate, and a nice one at that." He went on to tell me that once it was paid for and in my collection, I could call it anything I wanted too. We just both smiled as I reached into my pocket for a couple of twenties. The old phrase "A rose by any other name would smell as sweet" came to mind as I placed the point in my pocket and continued on with the show.

 I remember finding a corner-notched point shortly after I began collecting and bought my first typology book. Wanting to preserve as much of the artifact's history as I could on a note card, I neatly wrote the date, place of find, color, and size. The only line left to fill in was point type. "Simple enough," I thought, and grabbed my book. Two hours later, I had it narrowed down to one of six different types as I tossed the book onto the shelf, picked up the card and wrote "a nice one" on the line I had created asking for the type. In the last couple of decades I have had to force myself to study the various types from all over the country. It is hard to have an artifact sales and auction business and do authentications if you do not know the different traits associated with the points you are describing in print. I have found that one thing is clear and certain when using typology books, and to the frustrated new collector trying to use a 1,000+ page identification and value guide, I would just say this: While the general point style will get you close, it's the small traits that make the final determination. With some regions, the types are fewer and more varied and easier to type, while in others, such as Florida, many styles tend to look identical. This is when the little traits matter the most. Is the stem rounded or squared off? Does it constrict or expand? Does the eared area taper up or down? Noticing these little traits make a world of difference in correctly typing a relic.

The following are the general basal/hafting styles:

lanceolate	side notched	rounded base
bifurcated	corner notched	triangular
basal notched	stemmed	tang knives

PROJECTILE POINTS

While the type and style of projectile points being made in ancient times is quite varied depending on the time period, regional location, and other factors, their purpose remained the same — killing game. The concept of having a sharp weighted point attached to the end of a shaft which was projected either by hand or with the use of an atl-atl was the technology of the day. Projectile points served two purposes, both revolved around adding weight to the weapon. While a sharpened stick could easily penetrate an animal, when thrown, it lacked impact power. The added weight of a stone tip increased the impact power allowing the weapon to drive further into the animal's body and increasing the chance of striking a vital organ. The second purpose was to add weight to increase the distance a spear, dart, or arrow could travel.

Projectile points are categorized by collectors in many ways based on use, size, style, or age, but for the purpose of simplicity I have categorized them here based on the groups generally collected within the hobby.
- lances — used primarily on short distance spears or thrusting spears
- dart points — used in conjuction with an atl-atl spear thrower
- arrowpoints — projected by a bow
- birdpoints — smaller arrowpoints
- gempoints — high grade birdpoints

LANCES

The first projectile points were made to tip the ends of long lances during the Paleo period. These lances were used to thrust at, or to throw at, the animal being hunted. The use of long spears most likely continued throughout all the time periods as examples of this weapon could still be seen well into the historic.

Since quite often ancient man used the same style for knives and darts as well as lances, it can be hard to tell on some styles if a lanceolate tipped the end of a thrusting spear, was used as a dart point, or was hafted to a handle and used as a knife. As a general rule, I look for signs of ancient resharpening along the blade edges, and if present, I consider the item a knife. If a lanceolate is under 2" long, it could easily have either tipped a spear or a dart, and there really is no way to tell for absolute certain on these smaller lances.

3" Clovis made from Coastal Plains chert. Found in Jackson Co., Florida. Fluted on both faces. Collection of Cliff Jackson. $1,500.00.

Agate Basin made of Coshocton flint. Found in Clark Co., Kentucky. Collection of Donald Dix. Not listed.

PROJECTILE POINTS

2½" Plainview found in Howard Co., Missouri. Collection of John Selmer. $400.00.

3" Clovis found in Scioto Co., Ohio. Collection of Donald Dix. $2,200.00 – 2,400.00.

4¾" Hellgap made from Knife River flint. Found in Emmons Co., North Dakota. Collection of Larry Bumann. Personal find.

2¾" Agate Basin made from Knife River flint. Found in Emmons Co., North Dakota. Collection of Larry Bumann. Personal find.

PROJECTILE POINTS

2½" Plainview made from Burlington chert. Found in Madison Co., Illinois. Collection of Mike Denother. Personal find.

5" flint artifact made from Burlington chert. Found in Madison Co., Illinois. Collection of Mike Denother. Personal find.

3⁷⁄₈" Upper Mercer Paleo lance found in Franklin Co., Ohio. Collection of Mike Diano. $300.00.

3¹⁵⁄₁₆" Crowfield Clovis made of jasper. Found in Pennsylvania. Collection of Musée de la Neufve. Photo by Nicolas Tremblay. $525.00.

3½" Clovis made from Burlington. Found in Illinois. Collection of Musée de la Neufve. Photo by Nicolas Tremblay. $2,500.00.

PROJECTILE POINTS

Cumberland made of Ft. Payne. Found in Garrard Co., Kentucky. Collection of Randall Carrier. Not listed.

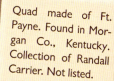

Quad made of Ft. Payne. Found in Morgan Co., Kentucky. Collection of Randall Carrier. Not listed.

Cumberland point found in Hart Co., Kentucky. Collection of Randall Carrier. Not listed.

2½" Beaver Lake made from Coshocton flint. It was found near Junction City in Perry Co., Ohio. Rob Dills collection. $200.00.

Cumberland point made of Ft. Payne. Found in Garrard Co., Kentucky. Collection of Randall Carrier. Not listed.

PROJECTILE POINTS

3³⁄₁₆" Paleo lance found in Ohio and made of Delaware. Rob Dills collection. $250.00.

4" Paleo Lanceolate found in Crawford Co., Ohio. Collection of Keith Ray. $350.00 – 400.00.

3⅛" Coshocton Paleo Lanceolate found in Pickaway Co., Ohio. Purchased from finder. Collection of Keith Ray. $175.00 – 200.00.

3¼" Paleo lance made from mottled Coshocton flint. Found in Richland Co., Ohio. Rob Dills collection. $450.00.

3⅛" Agate Basin found in Ohio. Made of Coshocton flint. Stem sides are ground over half way to the tip. Rob Dills collection. $500.00 – 600.00.

3½" parallel flaked Paleo lance found in Morrow Co., Ohio. Made of Flint Ridge chalcedony. Rob Dills collection. $600.00 – 800.00.

3¼" Agate Basin made of Burlington chert. Found in Madison Co., Illinois. Collection of Robert Denother. Personal find.

Browns Valley points. Center upper — River stained chert, Riley Co., Kansas. Center lower — Gray flint, from Rice, North Dakota. Upper left — Attica chert, Indiana. Lower left — olive-brown chert, Jasper Co., Indiana. Upper right — Galena chert, Henry Co., Illinois. Lower right — Colorado. Collection of Mike Kuchinski. $5,000.00+.

Clovis made from Dover. Found near Spring City, Tennessee. Collection of Rick Latell. $1,500.00 – 1,800.00.

2³⁄₁₆" Plainview made from a brownish chalcedony. Found on the Kansas River by Leavenworth, Kansas. Collection of Ron Van Heukelom. $600.00.

3⅛" Western Plains Paleo knife from the Folsom era. Made from a gray chalcedony. Collection of Ron Van Heukelom. $300.00 – 500.00.

3¹⁵⁄₁₆" Scottsbluff made from Edwards chert. Found in Texas. Collection of Rick Latell. $2,500.00.

Beaver Lake made from Dover chert. Found in Tennessee. Collection of Todd Walterspaugh. $3,500.00.

PROJECTILE POINTS

Flint Ridge Fluted Clovis found in Scioto Co., Ohio. Collection of Todd Walterspaugh. $3,000.00 – 3,800.00.

Pike County made from Fort Payne chert. Found in St. Francis Co., Arkansas. Collection of Todd Walterspaugh. $500.00.

3¾" Beaver Lake found in Kentucky. Made from Oolitchic chert. Collection of Peter Allen. $1,600.00.

Fluted Clovis made from Upper Mercer. Found on June 2, 1957, seven miles south of Upper Sandusky near Brownstown in Wyandot Co., Ohio. Collection of Todd Walterspaugh. $1,200.00 – 1,500.00.

3½" Early Eared made from Franciscan chert. Found in California. Collection of Peter Allen. $500.00.

DART POINTS

During the middle to late paleo period the invention of the atl-atl took over as the weapon of choice for native hunters. With its ability to launch a spear greater distances with increased impact power, the creation of atl-atl dart points to tip the spears of this new weapon had begun. As the atl-atl spear and dart system went on for over 10,000 years, the amount of projectile points created for this weapon system is staggering.

Sometimes it is hard to tell by size alone if a point was a knife exhausted by bifacial resharpening or a slightly larger dart point. Several such examples can be seen in these two frames of artifacts from the Steve Valentine collection.

Just as it can be hard telling with lanceolate style points if they were actually used as knives that were discarded or lost before much resharpening, the same problem can exist on some styles of notched points as again, certain styles of points were used both as knives as well as dart points. Again, it comes down to looking for signs of resharpening and comparing the width of the base to the length of the blade.

3" river stained Chattahootchie Dalton made from Coastal Plains chert. Found in Jackson CO., Florida. Collection of Cliff Jackson. $1,000.00.

Burlington Daltons. Left is 2¼" and the right is 2". From Missouri. Collection of Dennis Hess. $100.00 each.

Obsidian relic found in northern Nevada. Collection of Donald Dix. Personal find.

Elko Split Stem made of obsidian. Found in northern Nevada. Collection of Donald Dix. Personal find.

PROJECTILE POINTS

Eastgate Split Stem made of obsidian. Found in northern Nevada. Collection of Donald Dix. Personal find.

Agate artifact found in central Nevada. Collection of Donald Dix. Personal find.

Humboldt found in eastern Nevada. This early archaic atl-atl point was found in a dry lake bed where many paleo artifacts, such as clovis points and crescents, have been found over the years. Collection of Donald Dix. Personal find.

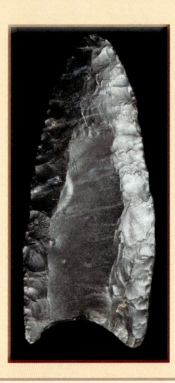

Clovis made from Coshocton flint. Found in Bourbon Co., Kentucky. Collection of Donald Dix. $2,800.00 – 3,200.00.

PROJECTILE POINTS

1½" Dart point made of Flint Ridge nethers. Found in Tuscarawas Co., Ohio. Collection of Edward Stevens. Not listed.

2" Serrated Stilwell. Found in Tuscarawas Co., Ohio. Collection of Edward Stevens. Personal find.

2" Archaic corner notch made from rare Flint Ridge with green swirls. Collection of Edward Stevens. Not listed.

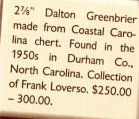

1⅛" multicolor jewel grade Flint Ridge point. Collection of Edward Stevens. Not listed.

2⅜" Hardaway Dalton made from rhyolite. Found in Lee Co., North Carolina. Collection of Frank Loverso. Personal find.

2⅞" Dalton Greenbrier made from Coastal Carolina chert. Found in the 1950s in Durham Co., North Carolina. Collection of Frank Loverso. $250.00 – 300.00.

1½" Hardaway made from black rhyolite. Found in Stanly Co., North Carolina. Collection of Frank Loverso. $250.00 – 300.00.

1⅜" Hardaway made from rhyolite. Found in Lee CO., North Carolina. Collection of Frank Loverso. Personal find.

PROJECTILE POINTS

1½" Hardaway made from rhyolite. Found in Durham Co., North Carolina. Collection of Frank Loverso. Personal find.

1⅝" Hardaway made of rhyolite. Found in Stanly Co., North Carolina. Collection of Frank Loverso. $250.00 – 300.00.

Flint artifact found in Monroe Co., Michigan. Collection of James Loughman. Personal find.

Group of Hardaways from North Carolina. Collection of Frank Loverso. $200.00 – 300.00 each.

Flint artifact found in Monroe Co., Michigan. Collection of James Loughman. Personal find.

PROJECTILE POINTS

2 3/16" Midland made from petrified wood. Found in New Mexico. Collection of John Selmer. $400.00 – 600.00.

1 3/8" Lake Erie Bifurcate found outside of Orrville in Wayne Co., Ohio, by Jerry Ray on 6-4-07. Collection of Keith Ray. $40.00 – 60.00.

1 1/2" Paleo point made from translucent Washington Pass agate. Found in Baca Co., Colorado. Collection of John Selmer. $750.00.

Flint artifact found in Monroe Co., Michigan. Collection of James Loughman. Personal find.

2 3/4" Adena made from Knife River flint. Found in Iowa. Collection of John Selmer. $125.00.

PROJECTILE POINTS

2⅜" Hanna made from Knife River flint. Found in South Dakota. Collection of John Selmer. $175.00.

1¾" Rio Grande made of petrified wood. Found in southern Colorado. Collection of John Selmer. $175.00.

2⁵⁄₁₆" Crowfield made from Pennsylvania jasper. Found in New Castle, Pennsylvania. Ancient damage to one ear. Collection of John Selmer. $1,500.00.

2" Eden found in New Mexico. Collection of John Selmer. Personal find.

2⅞" Black Mesa Narrow Neck made from mahogany obsidian. Found in New Mexico. Collection of John Selmer. Personal find.

PROJECTILE POINTS

1¼" Midland made from Knife River flint. Found in Fort Rice, North Dakota. Collection of John Selmer. $500.00.

1³⁄₁₆" Paleo Dart made of chalcedony, southeastern Colorado. Collection of John Selmer. $750.00.

1³⁄₁₆" point found in McLean Co., North Dakota. Collection of Larry Bumann. $200.00.

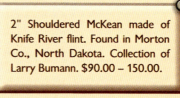

2" Shouldered McKean made of Knife River flint. Found in Morton Co., North Dakota. Collection of Larry Bumann. $90.00 – 150.00.

Paleo Dart made from red and yellow jasper. Found in the Columbia River Basin on 4/25/1959. Collection of John Selmer. $150.00.

1¾" Pelican Lake made of Knife River flint. Found in Mountrail Co., North Dakota. Collection of Larry Bumann. $90.00 – 150.00.

PROJECTILE POINTS

1¾" Knife River flint point found in Emmons Co., North Dakota. Collection of Larry Bumann. Personal find.

2" Knife River flint Pelican Lake point found in Emmons Co., North Dakota. Collection of Larry Bumann. Personal find.

1⅞" Pelican Lake made of Knife River flint. Found in Emmons Co., North Dakota. Collection of Larry Bumann. $90.00 – 150.00.

1¾" Pelican Lake made of silicified wood. Found in Mountrail Co., North Dakota. Collection of Larry Bumann. $150.00 – 200.00.

2⅛" Colby point made from Knife River flint. Found in Emmons Co., North Dakota. Collection of Larry Bumann. Personal find.

2⅜" Besant point made from Knife River flint. Found in Emmons Co., North Dakota. Collection of Larry Bumann. Personal find.

2¼" point made from Knife River flint. Found in Emmons Co., North Dakota. Collection of Larry Bumann. Personal find.

1¾" Besant knife made of Knife River flint. Found in Walworth Co., South Dakota. Collection of Larry Bumann. $90.00 – 150.00.

PROJECTILE POINTS

1¾" Oxbow made of petrified wood. Found in Mountrail Co., North Dakota. Collection of Larry Bumann. $150.00 – 250.00.

2 1/16" Duncan made of Knife River flint. Found in Mountrail Co., North Dakota. Collection of Larry Bumann. $90.00 – 110.00.

2 11/16" Duncan made of Knife River flint. Found in Kansas. Collection of Larry Bumann. $150.00 – 250.00.

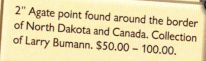

2" Agate point found around the border of North Dakota and Canada. Collection of Larry Bumann. $50.00 – 100.00.

Artifact found in Morton Co., North Dakota. Collection of Larry Bumann. Personal find.

1¾" Besant made from Knife River flint. Found in Mountrail Co., North Dakota. Collection of Larry Bumann. $75.00 – 100.00.

PROJECTILE POINTS

1½" Oxbow made from Knive River flint and found in North Dakota. Collection of Larry Bumann. $60.00 – 80.00.

1⅞" Shouldered McKean made of Knife River flint. Found in Sioux Co., North Dakota. Collection of Larry Bumann. $60.00 – 80.00.

1¾" Shouldered McKean made of Knife River flint. Found in Sioux Co., North Dakota. Collection of Larry Bumann. $90.00 – 150.00.

Front and back of 2¾" Pelican Lake made from Knife River flint. Found in Burleigh Co., North Dakota. $350.00 – 650.00.

PROJECTILE POINTS

1⅝" side notch made from Knife River flint and found in South Dakota. Collection of Larry Bumann. $60.00 – 80.00.

1⅞" Knife River flint artifact. Found in Mountrail Co., North Dakota. Collection of Larry Bumann. $100.00 – 200.00.

1½" Hanna made of Knife River flint. Found in Wyoming. Collection of Larry Bumann. $40.00 – 80.00.

1½" Midland found in Morton Co., North Dakota. Collection of Larry Bumann. Not listed.

1¾" Artifact made from agate. Found in Sioux Co., North Dakota. Collection of Larry Bumann. $50.00 – 100.00.

1½" Oxbow made of Knife River flint and found in North Dakota. Collection of Larry Bumann. Not listed.

1½" Oxbow made of Knife River flint and found in North Dakota. Collection of Larry Bumann. $80.00 – 100.00.

2" Midland made from Knife River flint. Found in Sioux Co., North Dakota. Collection of Larry Bumann. $750.00 – 1,000.00.

PROJECTILE POINTS

Flint artifact found in Red Deer River, Alberta. Collection of Lyle Guckert. Personal find.

Flint artifact found in Red Deer River, Alberta. Collection of Lyle Guckert. Personal find.

Flint artifact found in Red Deer River, Alberta. Collection of Lyle Guckert. Personal find.

1 5/16" Translucent Flint Ridge Intrusive Mound. Found in 2005 Zoar, Tuscarawas Co., Ohio. Personal find.

2 1/16" Transitional point made from Flint Ridge. Found in Perry Co., Ohio. Collection of Mike Diano. Personal find.

PROJECTILE POINTS

2¼" Upper Mercer Paleo stemmed point found in Ross Co., Ohio. Collection of Mike Diano. Personal find.

2" Paleo fluted point made from Delaware chert. Found in Fairfield Co., Ohio. Collection of Mike Diano. Personal find.

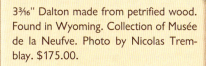

3³⁄₁₆" Dalton made from petrified wood. Found in Wyoming. Collection of Musée de la Neufve. Photo by Nicolas Tremblay. $175.00.

1¹³⁄₁₆" Holland found in Arkansas. Collection of Musée de la Neufve. $125.00.

Upper Mercer fluted point found in Fairfield Co., Ohio. Collection of Mike Diano. $450.00.

PROJECTILE POINTS

Arkabula made from Crowleys Ridge cobble chert. Found in Clay Co., Arkansas. Collection of Rick Stevens. $180.00 – 225.00.

Dalton made from Crowleys Ridge cobble chert. Found in Green Co., Arkansas. Collection of Rick Stevens. $100.00 – 125.00.

Allen point made from Reed Springs chert. Found in Osage Co., Oklahoma. Collection of Rick Stevens. $300.00 – 450.00.

San Patrice made from translucent agate. Found in 2008 in Osage Co., Oklahoma. One ear has been restored. Collection of Rick Stevens. Personal find.

PROJECTILE POINTS

3⁵⁄₁₆" Clovis made from Burlington. Found in Madison Co., Illinois. Collection of Robert Denother. Personal find.

2" Fluted Clovis made of a translucent material. Found in Ohio. Rob Dills collection. $300.00.

2¹⁄₁₆" Folsom found near Brule in Keith Co., Nebraska. Collection of Ron Van Heukelom. Not listed.

2" Midland made from a dark brown chalcedony. Found in Wyoming. Collection of Ron Van Heukelom. $300.00 – 500.00.

1¹³⁄₁₆" Midland found in Colorado City, Texas. Collection of Ron Van Heukelom. $800.00.

PROJECTILE POINTS

1⅝" Folsom made from banded obsidian. Found in New Mexico. Collection of Ron Van Heukelom. $1,500.00.

1¹³⁄₁₆" Midland made from Edwards Plateau chalcedony. Found in Terry Co., Texas. Collection of Ron Van Heukelom. $1,000.00.

Group of three serrated Archaic corner notched points. The center example is 2⅛". Found in Wheelersburg in Scioto Co., Ohio. Collection of Steve Valentine. Personal finds.

Pair of 1½" points found near Franklin Furnace in Scioto Co., Ohio. Both of these very nice points were found the same day in the same field. The point on the left is a fine example of an Archaic side notch and is made from a very high quality Flint Ridge jewel flint. The point on the right is a very nice Palmer made of Carter Cave flint. Collection of Steve Valentine. Personal finds.

Grouping of birdpoints that all measure around 1". These were al found on the same site near St. Paul, Kentucky. Collection of Steve Valentine. Personal finds.

PROJECTILE POINTS

Pair of 2¼" Kirk stemmed points found in Scioto Co., Ohio. Collection of Steve Valentine. Personal finds.

Group of bifurcated points foud in Lawrence Co., Ohio. Collection of Steve Valentine. Personal finds.

Exceptional Humboldt constricted base made from agate. Found in Warner Valley, Oregon. Collection of Terry & Loretta Clemens. Museum quality.

Flint artifact found in Stoddard Co., Missouri. Collection of Brandon McGowan. Personal find.

2" Oxbow made from Knife River flint. Found in North Dakota. Collection of Peter Allen. $250.00.

ARROWPOINTS

The current thought is that the bow and arrow weapon system first appeared at the end of the Woodland period, and brought with it the need for lighter, smaller projectile points. Ranging in size from approximately ½" to 2" long, true arrowpoints generally are narrower at the base than atl-atl points as the arrow shaft was much thinner than most atl-atl dart shafts.

Madison made of Boyle chert. Found in 1983 in Clark Co., Kentucky. Collection of Donald Dix. Not listed.

Desert Delta found in northern Nevada. Collection of Donald Dix. Personal find.

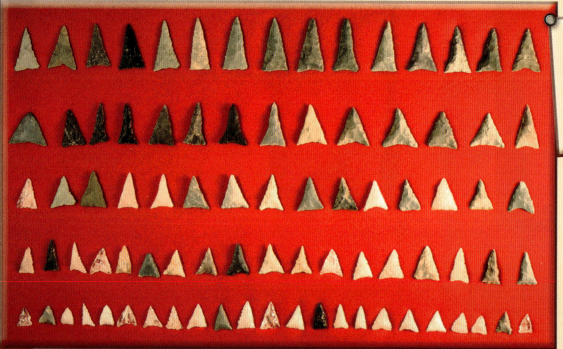

Group of Woodland triangles from various sites in North Carolina. The largest is 1½". Collection of Frank Loverso. Personal finds.

PROJECTILE POINTS

Yadkin points found in Durham Co., North Carolina. Collection of Frank Loverso. Personal finds.

Flint artifact found in Monroe Co., Michigan. Collection of James Loughman. Personal find.

Occaneechee and Yadkin. From various counties in North Carolina. Collection of Frank Loverso. Not listed.

PROJECTILE POINTS

Nice selection of Washita arrowpoints on display at the Museum of Native American Artifacts. Unlisted.

Nice selection of Sequoyah arrowpoints on display at the Museum of Native American Artifacts. Unlisted.

PROJECTILE POINTS

1⅞" Desert made from translucent petrified wood. Found in San Juan Co., New Mexico. Collection of John Selmer. $125.00.

1¾" Columbia Plateau made from translucent petrified wood. Found on the Columbia River in Washington. Collection of John Selmer. $500.00.

1⅞" Desert made from translucent petrified wood. Found in San Juan Co., New Mexico. Collection of John Selmer. $125.00.

1½" Desert side notch from Colorado. Collection of John Selmer. $75.00.

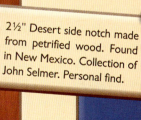

1³⁄₁₆" Desert with six notches. Found in Borger, Texas. Collection of John Selmer. $100.00.

1¹³⁄₁₆" Bitterroot made from Knife River flint. Found in Mountrail Co., North Dakota. Collection of John Selmer. $175.00.

2⅛" Desert side notch made from Alibates. Found in Baca Co., Colorado. Collection of John Selmer. $150.00.

2½" Desert side notch made from petrified wood. Found in New Mexico. Collection of John Selmer. Personal find.

2⅞" Desert side notch made from petrified wood. Found in New Mexico. Collection of John Selmer. Personal find.

PROJECTILE POINTS

2 1/16" Desert side notch made from translucent Washington Pass agate. Found in New Mexico. Collection of John Selmer. Personal find.

1 5/8" side notch made from translucent petrified wood. Found in New Mexico. Collection of John Selmer. Personal find.

2" side notch made from translucent petrified wood. Found in New Mexico. Collection of John Selmer. Personal find.

3/4" Desert double tip made from chalcedony. Found in Arizona. Collection of John Selmer. $200.00.

37mm Gunther made from yellow jasper. From Gold Beach, Oregon. Collection of Ken Gibson. $50.00.

Obsidian Gunther from Klamath Lake, Oregon. Left bard is professionally restored. Collection of Ken Gibson. Personal find.

33mm Gunther made from a light tan agate. Found in Rogue River, Oregon. Collection of Ken Gibson. $300.00.

28mm Gunther made from a dark red jasper. Found in Klamath Lake, Oregon. Collection of Ken Gibson. $225.00.

25mm jasper Gunther from Rogue River, Oregon. Collection of Ken Gibson. $350.00.

26mm jasper Gunther from Rogue River, Oregon. Collection of Ken Gibson. $175.00.

22mm jasper Gunther from Rogue River, Oregon. Collection of Ken Gibson. $175.00.

PROJECTILE POINTS

18mm jasper Gunther from Rogue River, Oregon. Collection of Ken Gibson. $150.00.

23mm agate Gunther from Klamath Lake, Oregon. Collection of Ken Gibson. $100.00.

Obsidian Gunther from Klamath Lake, Oregon. Collection of Ken Gibson. Personal find.

22mm jasper Gunther from Rogue River, Oregon. Collection of Ken Gibson. Not listed.

32mm red jasper Gunther from Rogue River, Oregon. Collection of Ken Gibson. $4,000.00.

32mm Gunther made from mottled chert. Found in Klamath Lake, Oregon. Collection of Ken Gibson. Not listed.

37mm Gunther from Gold Beach, Oregon. Collection of Ken Gibson. $250.00.

35mm agate Gunther from Klamath Lake, Oregon. Collection of Ken Gibson. $250.00.

37mm Gunther from Klamath Lake, Oregon. Collection of Ken Gibson. $150.00.

25mm Columbia Plateau found in Dalles, Oregon. Collection of Ken Gibson. $150.00.

23mm Columbia Plateau made from a light tan agate. Found on the Columbia River, Oregon. Collection of Ken Gibson. $100.00.

28mm Columbia Plateau made from red jasper. Found in Dalles, Oregon. Collection of Ken Gibson. $125.00.

PROJECTILE POINTS

27mm obsidian Gunther from Klamath Lake, Oregon. Collection of Ken Gibson. $80.00.

33mm jasper Shasta side notch from Klamath Lake, Oregon. Restored tip. Collection of Ken Gibson. Personal find.

31mm Columbia Plateau made from odsidian. Found in Grandview, Oregon. Collection of Ken Gibson. $100.00.

29mm Gunther made from red jasper. Found on Nightfire Island in northern California. Collection of Ken Gibson. $100.00.

24mm Gunther made from redish brown jasper. Found in the Rogue National Forest, California. Collection of Ken Gibson. $75.00.

Gunther from Klamath Falls, Oregon. Collection of Ken Gibson. $75.00.

31mm Gunther from Rogue River, Oregon. Collection of Ken Gibson. $200.00.

Nice selection of Eastgate arrowpoints on display at the Museum of Native American Artifacts. Unlisted.

PROJECTILE POINTS

30mm Shasta Gunther made of Franciscan chert. Found in northern California. Collection of Ken Gibson. $100.00.

28mm obsidian Eastgate from the Warner Valley, Oregon. Collection of Ken Gibson. $75.00.

18mm Columbia Plateau found in Washington. Collection of Ken Gibson. $125.00.

22mm Gunther from Applegate River, Oregon. Collection of Ken Gibson. $75.00.

27mm Columbia Plateau. Collection of Ken Gibson. $100.00.

27mm jasper Gunther from Klamath Lake, Oregon. Collection of Ken Gibson. $75.00 – 100.00.

21mm Columbia Plateau from John Day Rapids, Oregon. Collection of Ken Gibson. $300.00.

16mm Camus Valley found in Corvallis, Oregon. Collection of Ken Gibson. $150.00.

31mm jasper Gunther from Rogue River, Oregon. Collection of Ken Gibson. $500.00.

26mm jasper Gunther from Klamath Lake, Oregon. Collection of Ken Gibson. $150.00.

30mm jasper Gunther from Klamath Lake, Oregon. Collection of Ken Gibson. $150.00.

1 1/16" Gunther made from red jasper. Collection of Ken Gibson. $300.00.

PROJECTILE POINTS

30mm red jasper Gunther from Shady Cove, Oregon. Collection of Ken Gibson. $175.00.

42mm Gunther from Rogue River, Oregon. Collection of Ken Gibson. $150.00.

43mm Eastgate found in Burns, Oregon. Collection of Ken Gibson. $200.00.

27mm Gunther made from green jasper. Found in Florence, Oregon. Collection of Ken Gibson. $350.00.

45mm Columbia Plateau from the Columbia River, Oregon. Collection of Ken Gibson. $450.00.

44mm Gunther made from a light tan chert. Found in Florence, Oregon. Collection of Ken Gibson. $550.00.

1" artifact made of jasper. Found in Sioux Co., North Dakota. Collection of Larry Bumann. $50.00 – 80.00.

Pair of Bonito arrowpoints on display at the Museum of Native American Artifacts. Unlisted.

PROJECTILE POINTS

Nice selection of Caracara arrowpoints on display at the Museum of Native American Artifacts. Unlisted.

Nice selection of Caracara arrowpoints on display at the Museum of Native American Artifacts. Unlisted.

Plains triangle made of agate. Found in North Dakota. Collection of James White. $80.00.

1⅞" Scallorn corner notch found in Green Co., Missouri. Collection of Stephen Burks. Personal find.

PROJECTILE POINTS

Madison made from Burlington. Found in Webster Co., Missouri. Collection of Richard Eady. Personal find.

1½" to 1¾" Madison points found in Polk Co., Missouri. Collection of Steve Burks. $10.00 – 30.00.

1" to 1½" Madison points found in Polk Co., Missouri. Collection of Steve Burks. $15.00 – 25.00.

1¼" Plains side notched birdpoint made of agate. Found in Sioux Co., North Dakota. Collection of Larry Bumann. $35.00 – 50.00.

1¼" to 1¹¹⁄₁₆" Madison points from Madison Co., Illinois. Collection of Robert Denother. Personal finds.

PROJECTILE POINTS

BIRDPOINTS

These small arrowpoints are generally associated with the Mississippian time period and were once thought to have been used solely for the hunting of winged prey, a theory that has long ago been discarded. Birdpoints can be very well made and attractively flaked, and found in most all areas of occupation that utilized the bow and arrow.

1¼" to 1½" flint artifacts from southern Missouri. Collection of Stephen Burks. $15.00 – 50.00.

¾" to 1¾" Harrell birdpoints from Kay Co., Oklahoma. Collection of Stephen Burks. $25.00 – 100.00.

57

PROJECTILE POINTS

Scallorn found in Webster Co., Missouri. Collection of Richard Eady. $10.00 – 30.00.

Sequoyah points found in Webster Co., Missouri. Sizes range from ¾" to 1". Collection of Richard Eady. Personal find.

Scallorn points. Found in Webster Co., Missouri. Collection of Richard Eady. $10.00 – 30.00.

Scallorn made from Burlington. Found in Webster Co., Missouri. Collection of Richard Eady. Personal find.

Reed side notch made from Burlington. Found in Webster Co., Missouri. Collection of Richard Eady. Personal find.

Sequoyah and Scallorn birdpoints found Webster Co., Missouri. Collection of Richard Eady. Personal finds.

Sequoyah and Morrsi points found in Webster Co., Missouri. Sizes range from 1" to 1⅛". Collection of Richard Eady. Personal finds.

Sequoyah made from Burlington. Found in Greene Co., Missouri. Collection of Steve Burks. Personal find.

PROJECTILE POINTS

Serrated Sequoyah made from quartzite. Found in Polk Co., Missouri. Collection of Steve Burks. $20.00.

1½" Collins birdpoint found in Polk Co., Missouri. Collection of Steve Burks. $30.00.

Serrated Sequoyah and Scalorn points found in Polk Co., Missouri, on the same site. Collection of Steve Burks. $25.00 – 40.00.

GEMPOINTS

Gempoints are birdpoint-sized arrowpoints made from attractive high-grade material that are generally well flaked. Usually, the term "gempoint" is associated with the Pacific Northwest area but can apply to other locations as well. Many styles of gempoints are known to have been used for fishing along the Columbia River basin where they have been recovered for decades along the river's banks.

28mm agate Columbia Plateau from the Columbia River, Oregon. Collection of Ken Gibson. $75.00.

31mm agate Calopooya from the Fern Ridge Reservoir in Eugene, Oregon. Collection of Ken Gibson. $150.00.

25mm Columbia Plateau made from chalcedony. Found on the Columbia River, Oregon. Collection of Ken Gibson. $100.00.

30mm Calapooya found at the Fern Ridge Reservoir, Oregon. Collection of Ken Gibson. $125.00.

25mm Columbia Plateau from John Day Rapids, Oregon. Collection of Ken Gibson. $150.00.

25mm Columbia Plateau from Columbia River, Washington. Collection of Ken Gibson. $300.00.

29mm Gunther made from agate. Found on Nightfire Island, California. Collection of Ken Gibson. $200.00.

17mm Camus Valley made from translucent agate. Found in Corvallis, Oregon. Collection of Ken Gibson. $150.00.

20mm Columbia Plateau found on Sauvie's Island, Oregon. Collection of Ken Gibson. $100.00.

20mm agate Calapooya found in Corvallis, Oregon. Collection of Ken Gibson. $150.00.

24mm Columbia Plateau found in Wishram, Washington. Collection of Ken Gibson. $100.00.

35mm Gunther made from translucent agate. Found on the Hood River, Oregon. Collection of Ken Gibson. $250.00.

PROJECTILE POINTS

30mm Wallula made from multicolored agate. Found in Dalles, Oregon. Collection of Ken Gibson. $150.00.

29mm agate Gunther founding northern California. Collection of Ken Gibson. $200.00.

Wallula made from agate. Found in the late 1800s to early 1900s on the Columbia River between Portland and The Dalles. Collection of Kim Radke. $30.00.

Wallula Gap made of agate. Found on the Columbia River near the Tri-States. Collection of Kim Radke. $15.00 – 30.00.

Red quartz Desert Delta found n Sacramento, California. Collection of Mike Dolcini. Personal find.

Agate Toyah found in Texas. Collection of James White. $100.00.

PROJECTILE POINTS

Set of beautiful Agee gempoints. Museum of Native American Artifacts. Museum quality.

Nice selection of Gunther gempoints on display at the Museum of Native American Artifacts. Unlisted.

KNIVES AND BLADES

Knives made from flint are just as likely to be found as projectile points. A common misconception is that any hafted flaked relic under 2" is automatically a projectile point. This is not so — many examples can be seen of flint artifacts used as knives in sizes ranging from exceedingly larger to less than an inch long. Just as we have knives to suit many different purposes today, so did ancient man.

Knives of various styles are found at all areas of ancient occupation, and can range from full-sized "first stage" or unused condition to those that have been totally exhausted from repeated resharpening.

Many knives were hafted to a bone, wood, or antler handle, while others were designed and manufactured for direct hand-held use.

Some of the more common styles of knives collected are:

- Hand knives and blades
- Uniface and biface flake knives
- Hafted knives
- Tang knives
- Bi-pointed knives
- Crescent knives
- Square knives
- Four bevel knives

6" Adena knife found in Cass Co., Indiana. Great example of a full-size knife that was never subjected to a reduction in size from resharpening. Collection of John Lutz. Museum quality.

HAND KNIVES AND BLADES

This style of cutting tool was designed to be held in hand without the use of a handle. Thinner more ovate style hand knives are often referred to as blades by collectors.

6¼" knife made from patinated rhyolite. Found in Wake Co., North Carolina. Collection of Dave LoSapio. Personal find.

KNIVES AND BLADES

Paleo knife made from Upper Mercer flint. Found Feb. 29, 2004, in Stark Co., Ohio. Jeff Goodenow collection. Personal find.

4½" knife made from Coshocton. Found in Sego Bottom in Perry Co., Ohio. Collection of John Lutz. $40.00 – 60.00.

3⅝" knife made from Knife River flint. Found in South Dakota. Collection of John Selmer. $225.00 – 400.00.

3½" beveled Archaic knife made of Hartville Uplift moss jasper. One blade edge has a spokeshave. Found in Sweetwater Co., Wyoming. Collection of Kim Radke. $60.00 – 80.00.

KNIVES AND BLADES

2¾" knife made from agate. Found at the Boley site north of Mandan, North Dakota. Collection of Larry Bumann. $50.00 – 100.00.

2⅛" side knife made of Knife River flint and found in North Dakota. Collection of Larry Bumann. $150.00 – 250.00.

2⅞" knife made of Knife River flint and found in North Dakota. Collection of Larry Bumann. $50.00 – 100.00.

3" Paleo knife made of Knife River flint. Found in Morton Co., North Dakota. Collection of Larry Bumann. Personal find.

3" Knive River flint artifact found in North Dakota. Collection of Larry Bumann. Not listed.

KNIVES AND BLADES

2¾" side knife made from Knife River flint. Found in Burleigh Co., North Dakota. $350.00 – 650.00.

Flint artifact found in Red Deer River, Alberta. Collection of Lyle Guckert. Personal find.

4½" Paleo uniface knife made from Upper Mercer. Found in Highland Co., Ohio. Collection of Mike Diano. $200.00.

3¹⁵⁄₁₆" Paleo uniface blade made from Upper Mercer. Found in Fairfield Co., Ohio. Collection of Mike Diano. Personal find.

3⁹⁄₁₆" Upper Mercer fluted Paleo knife found in Licking Co., Ohio. Collection of Mike Diano. $300.00.

4" Covington found in Carroll Co., Arkansas. Collection of Mike Menichetti. Personal find.

Lerma blade made of Toronto chert. Found in Osage Co., Oklahoma. Collection of Rick Stevens. $275.00 – 325.00.

5⅛" Adena leaf blade made of Coshocton flint. And found in Ohio. Rob Dills collection. $300.00.

3¾" knife blade found in Gasconade Co., Missouri. John McCurdy collection. $65.00 – 85.00.

KNIVES AND BLADES

3⅝" by 2½" red ochre blade found in Ashland Co., Ohio. John McCurdy collection. $185.00 – 235.00.

3⁹⁄₁₆" knife blade found in Gasconade Co., Missouri. Made from Mozarkite flint. John McCurdy collection. $35.00 – 55.00.

7⅞" Cobbs made from Burlington. Found in St. Clair Co., Illinois. Collection of Rick Latell. $2,500.00 – 3,000.00.

KNIVES AND BLADES

3¾" thin Archaic blade made from Edwards Plateau chalcedony. Found in Coryell Co., Texas. Collection of Ron Van Heukelom. $500.00.

4⅝" knife made from Burlington. Found in Cedar Co., Missouri. Collection of Stephen Burks. $75.00.

2⅝" oval knife made from heat treated mozarkite. Found in Wright Co., Missouri. Collection of Stephen Burks. Personal find.

3⅝" Archaic blade found in Montgomery Co., Ohio, near Centerville. Collection of Steve Valentine. $100.00 – 150.00.

Coshocton knife found in Scioto Co., Ohio, near Franklin Furnace. Collection of Steve Valentine. Personal find.

KNIVES AND BLADES

4¼" oval knife made from mahogany obsidian. Found in the Great Basin. Collection of John Selmer. $400.00 – 600.00.

North blade made from Hornstone chert. Found in Benton Harbour, Michigan. Collection of Todd Walterspaugh. $500.00.

Rhyolite square back knife found in Pitt Co., North Carolina. Collection of Ron L. Harris. $75.00.

Flint artifact found in Stoddard Co., Missouri. Collection of Brandon McGowan. Personal find.

UNIFACE AND BIFACE FLAKE KNIVES

Knives that were made from large flakes and had a sharpened edge created by unifacial flaking along one or more edges are most commonly referred to as uniface knives; while knives made from large flakes that have bifacially flaked edges are generally called flake knives.

Examples of Uniface Knives

Group of Coshocton Uniface blades. The largest is 4". Collection of John Lutz. $50.00 – 100.00.

UNIFACE AND BIFACE FLAKE KNIVES

Pair of Paleo knives made from Flint Ridge and Burlington. Found in Anderson Co., Kentucky, and St. Louis Co., Illinois. Collection of Todd Walterspaugh. $400.00 for the pair.

4 9/16" Paleo uniface blade found in Fairfield CO., Ohio. Collection of Mike Diano. $150.00.

3½" leaf shaped uniface blades. Collection of John Lutz. $50.00 – 100.00.

73

UNIFACE AND BIFACE FLAKE KNIVES

Examples of Flake Knives

Rhyolite utilized flake knife found in Wilkes Co., North Carolina, near the Yadkin River. Collection of Ron L. Harris. $15.00.

3¼" flake knife found in Florida. Author's collection. $20.00 – 30.00.

Flake knife found in Ohio. Collection of Keith Ray. $80.00 – 100.00.

HAFTED KNIVES

Knives that were attached to a handle, regardless of the basal style are considered hafted knives. Used in all time periods in North America, hafted knives were attached to bone, wood, or antler handles, and quite often glued in place with pitch or asphaltum or a similar bonding substance before being tied with sinew or plant fibers.

4 5/16" Graham Cave made of Burlington chert. Found in Jersey Co., Illinois. Collection of Brad E Simmerman. Not listed.

3 3/8" corner notch found in St. Clair Co., Illinois. Collection of Brad E. Simmerman. $700.00 – 1,100.00.

5 5/8" knobbed base Hardin found in southeast Missouri. Collection of Brad E. Simmerman. Not listed.

HAFTED KNIVES

4 9/16" Hardin made of Burlington. Found in Macon Co., Missouri. Collection of Brad E. Simmerman. $1,500.00 – 2,500.00.

2 7/8" Snyders made of translucent mozarkite. Found July 15, 2008, in St. Clair Co., Missouri. Collection of Brad E. Simmerman. Personal find.

5 9/16" Dalton found in Carlyle Co., Kentucky. This point has a spokeshave in the blade. Collection of Carlos Black. $2,500.00.

3" Perkiomen made from yellow jasper. Found in the Connecticut River Valley, Massachusetts. Collection of Bruce Fenton. $300.00 – 400.00.

HAFTED KNIVES

4" Kirk corner notch made of a patinated rhyolite. Found in Durham Co., North Carolina. Collection of Cliff Jackson. $150.00.

4⅞" Little River made of petrified palm wood. Found in Marion Co., Texas. Collection of Carlos Black. Found along Big Cypress River in 1998. Personal find.

4" Archaic knife made from two-tone Edwards. Found in Colorado City, Texas. Collection of Cliff Jackson. $150.00 – 250.00.

3½" Marshall made of high grade Edwards. Found in Angelina Co., Texas. Collection of Cliff Jackson. $350.00 – 450.00.

HAFTED KNIVES

5" Delhi made of Edwards. Found in Angelina Co., Texas. Collection of Cliff Jackson. $500.00.

5" Ouachita made from Edwards. Found in San Janinto Co., Texas. Collection of Cliff Jackson. $500.00 – 750.00.

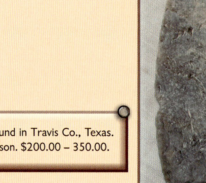

5" thin Friday knife made from Edwards. Found in Travis Co., Texas. Nice spattered patina. Collection of Cliff Jackson. $200.00 – 350.00.

6" Angostura knife made of Edwards. Found in Blanco Co., Texas. Found in two pieces in a bulldozer track. Patinated white. Collection of Cliff Jackson. $600.00 – 800.00.

HAFTED KNIVES

6" Angostura knife made of Edwards. Found in Blanco Co., Texas. Found in two pieces in a bulldozer track. Patinated white. Collection of Cliff Jackson. $500.00.

5 11/16" thin Friday made from Georgetown formation of Edwards Plateau. Found in Coke Co., Texas. Collection of Cliff Jackson. $1,500.00.

2 3/4" Paleo made from yellow quartz. Found in North Carolina. Collection of Cliff Jackson. $350.00.

4" river stained Hamilton stemmed made from Coastal Plains chert. Found in Flint River, Georgia. Collection of Cliff Jackson. $150.00.

HAFTED KNIVES

3½" Kirk serrated made from Coastal Plains chert. Found in Dale Co., Alabama. Collection of Cliff Jackson. $150.00.

4¾" Savannah River made from Coastal Plains chert. Found in Dale Co., Alabama. Collection of Cliff Jackson. $300.00.

5" Savannah River made from Coastal Plains chert. Found in Jackson Co., Florida. Collection of Cliff Jackson. $350.00.

3⅜" Elora made from Coastal Plains chert. Found in Chatham Co., Georgia. Collection of Cliff Jackson. $100.00.

4½" Morrow Mountain made from Coastal Plains chert. Found in Leon Co., Florida. Collection of Cliff Jackson. $400.00.

HAFTED KNIVES

Group of flint artifacts from Oklahoma and Missouri. Longest is 4¼". Collection of Cliff Jackson. $75.00 – 100.00 each.

3⅝" Kirk made from heat-treated variegated Burlington. Found in Boone Co., Missouri. Collection of Cliff Jackson. $150.00.

4" Dalton made from variegated Burlington. Found in Boone Co., Missouri. Collection of Cliff Jackson. $500.00.

HAFTED KNIVES

4¾" Krieger made of Red Springs chert from Oklahoma. Collection of Cliff Jackson. $400.00.

5½" Burlington Adena blade from Kaw River, Kansas. Collection of Cliff Jackson. $250.00.

4⅝" Krieger made from Ouachita quartzite. Found in Arkansas. Has an extra notch in blade edge for sturdier hafting. Collection of Cliff Jackson. $150.00 – 200.00.

5½" Stanfield made from Red Springs chert. From Dequeen, Arkansas. Collection of Cliff Jackson. $300.00 – 500.00.

HAFTED KNIVES

5⅝" Gary made from Keokuk. Found in Northeastern Oklahoma. Collection of Cliff Jackson. $500.00.

2½" Kirk serrated made from Horstone. Found in Perry Co., Indiana. Collection of Dennis Hess. $100.00.

Lost Lakes. The right example is 3" and made from Dover. The left is made from Fort Payne. Collection of Dennis Hess. $100.00 each.

Plateau Pentagonal found in Central Nevada. In the 1800s the Mormons were in fear of being invaded by the US Army for some of their religious practices. They decided to do an extensive exploration of the deserts to the west (Nevada) to search out possible hiding places. In their journals of this exploration they mentioned a tribe of natives in central Nevada, near Golconda, known as the White Knives due to their distinctive white knives. After several camping trips in the area I found this white knife. The tip was poking out of the bottom of a sage brush. I picked up the tip and when I looked down again there was there was base. Glued back together it looks pretty good. Don Dix, collector. Personal find.

HAFTED KNIVES

Wilits side notch made of agate. Found in a sand dune in western Nevada about 20 miles from the California state line. Collection of Donald Dix. Personal find.

Adena vanishing stem made from Boyle chert. Found during the excavation for a subdivision off Barns Mill Rd. in Madison Co., Kentucky. Collection of Donald Dix. Personal find.

Heavy duty found in Clark Co., Kentucky. Collection of Donald Dix. $100.00 – 150.00.

Pine Tree made from Boyle chert. Found in Clark Co., Kentucky. Collection of Donald Dix. $150.00 – 200.00.

Stemmed Kirk made of Carter Cave flint. Found in Clark Co., Kentucky. Collection of Donald Dix. $100.00 – 200.00.

HAFTED KNIVES

Cobbs made from Boyle chert. Found in Clark Co., Kentucky. Collection of Donald Dix. $150.00 – 250.00.

Indented base Dovetail made from Breathitt chert. Found in Clark Co., Kentucky. Breathitt cherts usage was almost entirely limited to the manufacture of rough flint celts, adzes, and gouges. Collection of Donald Dix. $800.00 – 1,000.00.

Heavy duty found in Woodford Co., Kentucky. Collection of Donald Dix. $125.00 – 150.00.

4 7/16" Cody Complex Paleo knife made from translucent Washington Pass agate. Found in western Colorado. Collection of John Selmer. $3,500.00.

HAFTED KNIVES

Clipped Wing Dovetail made from Carter Cave flint. Found in Clark Co., Kentucky. Collection of Donald Dix. $500.00 – 700.00.

Pine Tree found in Jessamine Co., Kentucky, in a tobacco field on 5/8/2008. Collection of Donald Dix. Personal find.

Pine Tree found in Jessamine Co., Kentucky, in 2006. Collection of Donald Dix. Personal find.

3" Lost Lake found in Jessamine Co., Kentucky, in 1968. Collection of Donald Dix. $800.00.

HAFTED KNIVES

1⅞" highly translucent Flint Ridge e-notch. Edward Stevens collection. Not listed.

1⅞" Hopewell made of Flint Ridge nethers. Collection of Edward Stevens. Not listed.

1½" Flint Ridge pentagonal with a clear quartz inclusion running from the tip to the base. Collection of Edward Stevens. Not listed.

3¼" Hopewell made of Flint Ridge nethers. Collection of Edward Stevens. Not listed.

6¼" Morrow Mountain made from green rhyolite. Found in North Hampton Co., North Carolina. Collection of Frank Loverso. Not listed.

87

HAFTED KNIVES

Group of North Carolina artifacts including Kirks, Morrow Mountian, Guilford, and Stanly. Collection of Frank Loverso. Most are personal finds.

5½" thin Morrow Mountain made from rhyolite. Found in Durham Co., North Carolina. Collection of Frank Loverso. Personal find.

3⅞" Rowan made from rhyolite. Found in Granville Co., North Carolina. Collection of Frank Loverso. Personal find.

HAFTED KNIVES

3⅜" serrated Kirk made from green rhyolite. Found in Western North Carolina. Collection of Frank Loverso. $250.00 – 300.00.

5⅝" rhyolite point found in Durman Co., North Carolina. ¼" restoration to the tip. Collection of Frank Loverso. Personal find.

5⅛" green rhyolite point found in Durham Co., North Carolina. Collection of Frank Loverso. Personal find.

Fluted Paleo found in Wayne Co., Ohio, in December of 2008. Collection of Tayler Wharton. Personal find.

HAFTED KNIVES

Flint artifact found in Monroe Co., Michigan. Collection of James Loughman. Personal find.

2 5/8" Newnan made from coral. Found in Marion Co., Florida. Collection of James White. $400.00.

2 1/2" Hernando made from Coast chert. Found in Marion Co., Florida. Collection of James White. $500.00.

2 9/16" Hernando made from Coast chert. Found in Marion Co., Florida. Collection of James White. $500.00.

3 3/8" Adena made from Hixton quartzite. Found in Wisconsin. Collection of James White. $500.00.

HAFTED KNIVES

Flint Ridge and Glacial Drift pentagonals found in Portage Co., Ohio. Jeff Adams collection. Personal find.

Upper Mercer Ashtabula found in Ohio. Jeff Adams collection. Not listed.

Flint Ridge Meadowood found in Ohio. Jeff Adams collection. Not listed.

Upper Mercer bevel found in Portage Co., Ohio. Jeff Adams collection. Personal find.

Upper Mercer corner notch found in Portage Co., Ohio. Jeff Adams collection. Personal find.

HAFTED KNIVES

Upper Mercer base notch found in Portage Co., Ohio. Jeff Adams collection. Personal find.

Flint Ridge side notch found in Portage Co., Ohio. Jeff Adams collection. Personal find.

5" Onondoga corner notch found in Portage Co., Ohio. Jeff Adams collection. Not listed.

5¾" Flint Ridge Dovetail. Found in Mahoning Co., Ohio. Jeff Adams collection. Not listed.

HAFTED KNIVES

4½" MacCorkle made of Upper Mercer. Found in Franklin Co., Ohio. Jeff Adams collection. Not listed.

Midwest Hemphill. Jeff Goodenow collection. $100.00 – 150.00.

4½" Riverstained Meadowood. Found in Belmont Co., Ohio. Collection of John Lutz. $300.00 – 400.00.

4¾" Adena Beavertail Made from hornstone. Collection of John Lutz. $300.00 – 500.00.

HAFTED KNIVES

3¾" uniface knife made from Flint Ridge flint. Found in Fairfield Co., Ohio. Collection of John Lutz. $75.00 – 150.00.

Adena made from Burlington. Found in Montgomery Co., Missouri. Collection of John Ray. Personal find.

3¾" Snyders made from hornstone. Collection of John Lutz. $400.00 – 600.00.

Sedalia made from Burlington. Found in Lincoln Co., Missouri. Collection of John Ray. Personal find.

Point made from Burlington. Found in Lincoln Co., Missouri. Collection of John Ray. Personal find.

Wadlow blade made from Burlington. Found in Lincoln Co., Missouri. Collection of John Ray. Personal find.

HAFTED KNIVES

Sedalia made from Burlington. Found in Lincoln Co., Missouri. Collection of John Ray. Personal find.

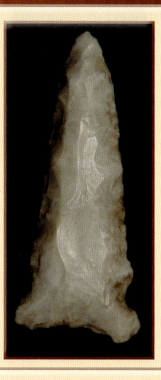

Grahm Cave made from Burlington. Found in Lincoln Co., Missouri. Collection of John Ray. Personal find.

Angostra made from Burlington. Found in Lincoln Co., Missouri. Collection of John Ray. Personal find.

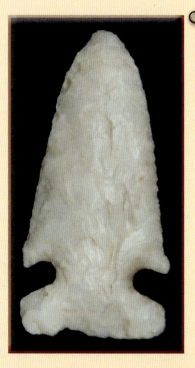

Point made from Burlington. Found in Lincoln Co., Missouri. Collection of John Ray. Personal find.

Sloan Dalton blade made from Burlington. Found in Lincoln Co., Missouri. Collection of John Ray. Personal find.

HAFTED KNIVES

Point made from Burlington. Found in Lincoln Co., Missouri. Collection of John Ray. Personal find.

Adena made from Burlington. Found in Lincoln Co., Missouri. Collection of John Ray. Personal find.

Adena made from Burlington. Found in Lincoln Co., Missouri. Collection of John Ray. Personal find.

Dalton made from Burlington. Found in Lincoln Co., Missouri. Collection of John Ray. Personal find.

Dalton Holland made from Burlington. Found in Lincoln Co., Missouri. Collection of John Ray. Personal find.

Classic Snyders found in Lincoln Co., Missouri. Thin and translucent. Collection of John Ray. Personal find.

3" Dovetail made from Hornstone. Found in Harrison Co., Indiana. Collection of John Selmer. $500.00.

3 1/16" Dovetail made from Dover. Found in Kentucky. Collection of John Selmer. $425.00.

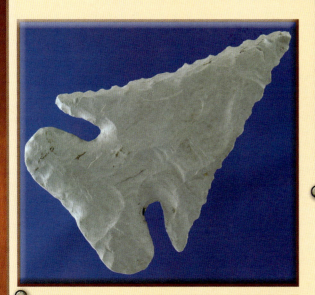

3" Thebes from Ohio. Collection of John Selmer. $425.00.

3 1/4" Dovetail made of Hornstone. Found in Kentucky. Collection of John Selmer. $400.00.

HAFTED KNIVES

3 3/16" corner notch made from obsidian. Found in New Mexico. Collection of John Selmer. Personal find.

3 1/4" Lost Lake made from Upper Mercer. Found in Ohio. Collection of John Selmer. $750.00.

4 1/4" Great Basin oval knife made from mahogany obsidian. Collection of John Selmer. $400.00.

2 3/8" Holland made from Mayes Creek. Found in Pike Co., Illinois. Collection of John Selmer. $250.00.

HAFTED KNIVES

3¾" Greenbriar Dalton made of Dover. Found in Barkley Lake, Kentucky. Collection of John Selmer. $900.00.

3⅛" Thebes made from Coshocton flint. Found in Licking Co., Ohio. Collection of John Selmer. $300.00.

3¾" double notched Dovetail made from Flint Ridge. Found in Ohio. Collection of John Selmer. $1,000.00.

3¾" wide base Dovetail made from Burlington. Found in St. Louis Co., Illinois. Collection of John Selmer. $750.00.

HAFTED KNIVES

2¼" Decatur made from hornstone. Found in Kentucky. Hafted scraper with a purposeful flute to create a chiseled tip. Collection of John Selmer. $200.00.

3⁵⁄₁₆" Lost Lake with Spokeshave. Made from Hornstone and found in Kentucky. Collection of John Selmer. $750.00.

3¼" Thebes made from Bayport. Found in Bartholomew Co., Indiana. Collection of John Selmer. $600.00.

3⁹⁄₁₆" deep notch Lost Lake made from Sonora. Found in Logan Co., Kentucky. Collection of John Selmer. $2,500.00.

HAFTED KNIVES

3⅛" Thebes found in Franklin Co., Ohio. Collection of John Selmer. $450.00.

2⅝" Scottsbluff made of Knife River flint from the Northern High Plains. Collection of John Selmer. $750.00.

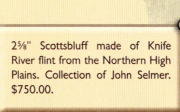

4 3/16" Lost Lake made of hornstone. Found in Kanawha Co., West Virginia. Collection of John Selmer. $2,000.00.

4 9/16" Archaic deep notch made from Coshocton flint. Found in Holmes Co., Ohio. Collection of John Selmer. $900.00.

HAFTED KNIVES

2³⁄₁₆" corner notch made of Coshocton flint. Found in Ashalnd Co., Ohio. Collection of Keith Ray. $100.00 – 150.00.

3⁵⁄₈" Thebes made of Coshocton flint. Found in Knox Co., Ohio. Collection of Keith Ray. $300.00 – 500.00.

3³⁄₈" notched base Dovetail made of Coshocton flint. Found in Hamilton Co., Ohio. Collection of Keith Ray. $375.00 – 425.00.

3¹⁄₁₆" micro notch made of Coshocton flint. Found in Ohio. Collection of Keith Ray. $250.00 – 300.00.

2½" Archaic side notch made of Coshocton flint. Found in Mercer Co., Ohio. Collection of Keith Ray. $60.00 – 80.00.

3⅛" Thebes found Nov. 23, 1937, in Butler Co., Ohio. Collection of Keith Ray. $375.00 – 400.00.

3⅞" Adena made from Flint Ridge. Found in Licking Co., Ohio. Collection of Keith Ray. $350.00 – 375.00.

3½" Archaic point found in Highland Co., Ohio. Collection of Keith Ray. $175.00 – 200.00.

2⅝" MacCorkle made of Coshocton flint. Found in Hardin Co., Ohio. Collection of Keith Ray. $300.00 – 350.00.

2⅞" MacCorkle made from Coshocton flint. Found in Crawford Co., Ohio. Collection of Keith Ray. $150.00 – 175.00.

HAFTED KNIVES

2⅞" pentagonal knife made from agate. Found in the Alvord Desert, Oregon. Collection of Ken Gibson. $200.00.

4½" Dalton found in Pettis Co., Missouri. Collection of Kent Langreder. Personal find.

4⅛" Knife River flint point found in Morton Co., North Dakota. Broken and glued. Collection of Larry Bumann. Personal find.

3" Besant made from Knife River flint. Found in Emmons Co., North Dakota. Collection of Larry Bumann. Personal find.

HAFTED KNIVES

3¼" knife made from Knife River flint. Found in North Dakota. Collection of Larry Bumann. $70.00 – 100.00.

3¼" Middle Archaic knife made of Knife River flint and found in North Dakota. Collection of Larry Bumann. Not listed.

3" Kirk corner notch point made of Knife River flint. Found in eastern North Dakota. Collection of Larry Bumann. $150.00 – 250.00.

4⅛" Knife River flint point found in North Dakota. Collection of Larry Bumann. $400.00 – 750.00.

3½" beveled knife made from Knife River flint. Found in Sioux Co., North Dakota. Collection of Larry Bumann. $150.00 – 250.00.

HAFTED KNIVES

2⅝" base tang knife made from Knife River flint. Found in Sioux Co., North Dakota. Collection of Larry Bumann. Not listed.

Patinated Knife River flint point found in Emmons Co., North Dakota. Not listed.

4⅜" Ft. Ancient knife found in Sylvania, Ohio. Found in a sand pile at a construction site. Collection of Jim & Nancy Loughman. Museum quality.

Flint artifact found in Red Deer River, Alberta. Collection of Lyle Guckert. Personal find.

HAFTED KNIVES

2 7/16" Jewl Flint Ridge e-notch. Found in 1992, Massillon, Stark Co., Ohio. Mark Gram collection. Personal find.

2 5/16" flint artifact made from Burlington. Found in Madison Co., Illinois. Collection of Mike Denother. Personal find.

2 9/16" Ferry. Found in Madison Co., Illinois. Collection of Mike Denother. Personal find.

3 5/8" Steuben. Found in Madison Co., Illinois. Collection of Mike Denother. Personal find.

2 1/4" flint artifacts made from Burlington. Found in Madison Co., Illinois. Collection of Mike Denother. Personal find.

2 7/8" stemmed point found in Madison Co., Illinois. Collection of Mike Denother. Personal find.

HAFTED KNIVES

3 11/16" Kramer made from Burlington chert. Found in Madison Co., Illinois. Collection of Mike Denother. Personal find.

4¾" Stanfield made from Logan Co. chert. Found in Ashland Co., Ohio. Collection of Mike Diano. $300.00.

3½" Meadowood made from Upper Mercer. Found in Perry Co., Ohio. Collection of Mike Diano. $250.00.

2½" notched base point made from Upper Mercer. Found in Franklin Co., Ohio. Collection of Mike Diano. $150.00 – 250.00.

3¾" Stanfield made from Flint Ridge flint. Found in Franklin Co., Ohio. Collection of Mike Diano. $150.00.

HAFTED KNIVES

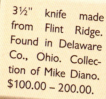
3½" knife made from Flint Ridge. Found in Delaware Co., Ohio. Collection of Mike Diano. $100.00 – 200.00.

2¼" diagonal notch made from Flint Ridge. Beveled with heavy base grinding. Found in Franklin Co., Ohio. Collection of Mike Diano. Not listed.

2½" Archaic bevel made from Upper Mercer. Found in Pickaway Co., Ohio. Collection of Mike Diano. $125.00 – 175.00.

4¼" Nellie stemmed lance found in Coshocton Co., Ohio. Collection of Mike Diano. $200.00.

4¼" Upper Mercer Cache blade found in Perry Co., Ohio. Collection of Mike Diano. $200.00.

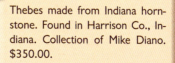

Thebes made from Indiana hornstone. Found in Harrison Co., Indiana. Collection of Mike Diano. $350.00.

HAFTED KNIVES

4" Upper Mercer stemmed lance found in Perry Co., Ohio. Collection of Mike Diano. $200.00.

2¾" stemmed lance made from upper Mercer. Found in Perry Co., Ohio. Collection of Mike Diano. $100.00.

1¾" exhausted wide base Dovetail made from Flint Ridge. Found in Pickaway Co., Ohio. Collection of Mike Diano. Personal find.

3¼" serrated heavy duty made from Upper Mercer. Found in Franklin Co., Ohio. Collection of Mike Diano. $200.00.

2¼" heavy duty made from Indiana hornstone. Found in Franklin Co., Ohio. Collection of Mike Diano. $85.00 – 125.00.

HAFTED KNIVES

2½" wide base Dovetail made from Upper Mercer. Found in Perry Co., Ohio. Collection of Mike Diano. Personal find.

3¾" upper Mercer Paleo blade found in Richland Co., Ohio. Collection of Mike Diano. $200.00.

Agate Rogue knife found in Jackson Co., Oregon. Collection of Mike Dolcini. $400.00.

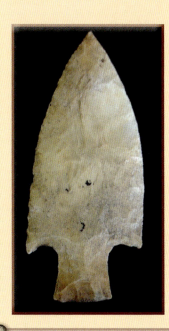

3" Hopewell found in Barry Co., Missouri. Collection of Mike Menichetti. Personal find.

3" beveled Searcy made of mozarkite flint. Found in Carroll Co., Arkansas, along the banks of the White River. Collection of Mike Menichetti. Personal find.

HAFTED KNIVES

2½" Lost Lake made from Dover chert. Found in Hardin Co., Tennessee. Collection of Musée de la Neufve. $300.00 – 450.00.

Adena Dickson found in Barry Co., Missouri, along the eroded shore of a man-made lake. Collection of Mike Menichetti. Personal find.

Holland made of Boone chert. Found in Barry Co., Missouri, along the eroded shore of a man-made lake. Collection of Mike Menichetti. Personal find.

2½" Pickwick made of Fort Payne chert. Found in Tennessee. Collection of Musée de la Neufve. Photo by Nicolas Tremblay. Not listed.

3⅛" Robbins made from Coshocton. Found in Summit Co., Ohio. Collection of Musée de la Neufve. $50.00.

HAFTED KNIVES

4 7/16" Coshocton Dovetail found in Clark Co., Ohio. Collection of Keith Ray. $1,200.00 – 1,400.00.

3 9/16" Little Bear Creek made from Buffalo River chert. Found in Hardin Co., Tennessee. Collection of Musée de la Neufve. $175.00.

3 11/16" Adena made from hornstone. Found in Kentucky. Collection of Musée de la Neufve. $125.00 – 200.00.

2 9/16" Greenbrier made from Buffalo River chert. Found in Tennessee. Collection of Musée de la Neufve. $300.00.

HAFTED KNIVES

4¾" Paleo knife made from Coshocton. Found in Coshocton Co., Ohio. Collection of Musée de la Neufve. Photo by Nicolas Tremblay. $450.00 – 500.00.

2⅜" Dovetail made from Flint Ridge. Found in Ohio. Collection of Musée de la Neufve. Photo by Nicolas Tremblay. $225.00.

2½" Thebes made from Zaleski flint. Found in Ohio. Collection of Musée de la Neufve. $175.00.

4¾" Big Sandy made of Dover chert. Found in Benton Co., Tennessee. Collection of Musée de la Neufve. $750.00.

HAFTED KNIVES

Fractured base point made of Ft. Payne. Found in Garrard Co., Kentucky. Collection of Randall Carrier. Not listed.

Sonora knobbed Hardin found in central Kentucky. Collection of Randall Carrier. Not listed.

Dovetail found in Boyle Co., Kentucky. Collection of Randall Carrier. Not listed.

Carter Cave Decatur found in southern Indiana. Collection of Randall Carrier. Not listed.

Pulaski Co., Kentucky, flint artifact. Collection of Randall Carrier. Not listed.

Ft. Payne blade found in Mercer Co., Kentucky. Collection of Randall Carrier. Not listed.

HAFTED KNIVES

Lost Lake made of Ft. Payne. Found in Garrard Co., Kentucky. Collection of Randall Carrier. Not listed.

Dovetail made of Sonora flint. Found in Hardin Co., Kentucky. Collection of Randall Carrier. Not listed.

Adena vanishing stem made of Sonora flint. Found in central Kentucky. Collection of Randall Carrier. Not listed.

Knobbed Hardin made of Sonora. Found in 1957 near the Salt River in western Boyle Co., Kentucky. Collection of Randall Carrier. Not listed.

Williams found in 2005 in Clay Co., Arkansas. Collection of Rick Stevens. Personal find.

HAFTED KNIVES

Jacks Reef made from Niobrara jasper. Found in Kay Co., Oklahoma. Collection of Rick Stevens. $100.00 – 125.00.

Scottsbluff made of Florence chert. Found in Osage Co., Oklahoma. Collection of Rick Stevens. $200.00 – 250.00.

Gary Point made from white Boone chert. Found in Sequoyah Co., Oklahoma. Collection of Rick Stevens. $40.00 – 80.00.

Cache River made from Crowleys Ridge cobble chert. Found in 2006 in Clay Co., Arkansas. Collection of Rick Stevens. Personal find.

Thin Dunn point made from white Boone chert. Found in Sequoyah Co., Oklahoma. Collection of Rick Stevens. $100.00 – 125.00.

HAFTED KNIVES

Hidden Valley made from white Boone chert. Found in Sequoyah Co., Arkansas. Collection of Rick Stevens. $125.00 – 175.00.

Scottsbluff made from mozarkite. Found in 2008 in Osage Co., Oklahoma. Collection of Rick Stevens. Personal find.

3⅝" pentagonal knife found in Scioto Co., Ohio. Large for the type. Collection of Keith Ray. $250.00 – 300.00.

3⅛" heavily patinated Coshocton E-Notch found in Ohio. Collection of Keith Ray. $400.00 – 450.00.

3 7/16" constricted base Thebes made of Flint Ridge flint. Found in Licking Co., Ohio. Rob Dills collection. $500.00 – 600.00.

HAFTED KNIVES

2 15/16" notch base made of Coshocton flint and found in Stark Co., Ohio. Rob Dills collection. $200.00 – 300.00.

2 1/8" notch base point made of Coshocton flint and found in Ohio. Rob Dills collection. $125.00 – 175.00.

3 1/16" notch base made from Coshocton flint and found in Ohio. Rob Dills collection. $300.00 – 400.00.

2 7/8" Coshocton notch base. Found in Madison Twp., Licking Co., Ohio. Rob Dills collection. $250.00 – 350.00.

3 1/8" notch base made from Coshocton. Base found in Portage Co., Ohio near Hiram College by Ed Stevens in 1988. Rob Dills collection. $300.00 – 400.00.

4 1/2" notch base made from Coshocton flint. Found in the early 1900s in Hamilton Co., Ohio, near Colombia Parkway. Rob Dills collection. $800.00 – 1,200.00.

HAFTED KNIVES

3" transitional stemmed point made of Coshocton flint and found in Ohio. Rob Dills collection. $150.00.

3" Coshocton Meadowood found in Ohio. Rob Dills collection. $100.00.

2 11/16" Archaic pentagonal made from Zeleski flint. Found in Delaware Co., Ohio. Rob Dills collection. $175.00.

2 3/8" basal notch made from Coshocton flint and found in Holmes Co., Ohio. Rob Dills collection. $150.00.

2 9/16" Intrusive Mound made from Coshocton flint and found in Ohio. Rob Dills collection. $150.00.

3 1/8" heavy duty point made from Zaleski flint. Found in Cuyahoga Co., Ohio. Rob Dills collection. $200.00.

HAFTED KNIVES

3¾" Coshocton Decatur found in Knox Co., Ohio. Rob Dills collection. $400.00.

4" Archaic side notch made from Coshocton flint. Found in Muskingum Co., Ohio, near Chandlersville. Rob Dills collection. $400.00.

4⅞" Hopewell made from Coshocton flint and found in Ohio. Rob Dills collection. $350.00.

2¹³⁄₁₆" Dovetail made from Flint Ridge chalcedony and found in Ohio. Rob Dills collection. $300.00.

3¹⁄₁₆" beveled Dovetail made of Flint Ridge flint. Found in Licking Co., Ohio. Rob Dills collection. $400.00.

121

HAFTED KNIVES

3½" Dovetail made from Flint Ridge flint. Found in Delaware Co., Ohio. Rob Dills collection. $600.00.

2½" Flint Ridge Dovetail found in Licking Co., Ohio. Found near Buckeye Lake. Rob Dills collection. $300.00.

3" medium base Dovetail made of Flint Ridge moss agate. Found in Summit Co., Ohio, in 1928. Rob Dills collection. $400.00.

2½" button base Dovetail made of Flint Ridge flint. Found in Ross Co., Ohio. Rob Dills collection. $600.00.

4 1/16" button base Dovetail made of Flint Ridge flint and found in Ohio. Rob Dills collection. $1,000.00.

HAFTED KNIVES

3½" opposing notch Dovetail made of Flint Ridge flint. Found in Delaware Co., Ohio. Rob Dills collection. $700.00.

4⅞" hip roof base Dovetail found in Ohio. Made of Flint Ridge flint. Rob Dills collection. $2,500.00.

3½" Dovetail made of Flint Ridge flint. Found in Perry Co., Ohio. Rob Dills collection. $700.00.

3¼" Flint Ridge Dovetail found in Richland Co., Ohio. Rob Dills collection. $650.00.

HAFTED KNIVES

2½" Big Sandy made of two-tone Coshocton flint. Found in Coshocton Co., Ohio. Rob Dills collection. $150.00.

2 5/16" Intrusive Mound made of Coshocton flint. Found in Ohio. Rob Dills collection. $150.00.

4 7/8" Adena made of Coshocton flint. Found in Ohio. Rob Dills collection. $300.00.

3 15/16" Archaic side notch made of Coshocton flint. Found in Union Co., Ohio. Rob Dills collection. $250.00.

4 1/16" Ashtabula made of Coshocton flint. Found in Ashland Co., Ohio. Rob Dills collection. $400.00.

3 1/8" Archaic corner notch made of Coshocton flint. Found in Ohio. Rob Dills collection. $350.00.

HAFTED KNIVES

2⅞" Bottleneck made of Jem Flint Ridge flint. Found in Ashland Co., Ohio. Rob Dills collection. $300.00.

3⅛" Bottleneck made of Gem Flint Ridge flint. Found in Ohio. Rob Dills collection. $400.00.

2¾" unfluted Clovis made of Coshocton flint. Found in Wyandot Co., Ohio. Rob Dills collection. $300.00.

3 1/16" stemmed lance found in Crawford Co., Ohio. Rob Dills collection. $350.00.

3⅞" Ohio Stringtown lance. Made of Nellie chert. Rob Dills collection. $600.00.

4⅛" wide base Dovetail made from Carter Cave flint and found in Kentucky. Collection of Keith Ray. $250.00 – 300.00.

HAFTED KNIVES

2¾" Stringtown lance found in Ohio. Made of Nellie chert. Rob Dills collection. $400.00.

3³⁄₁₆" stemmed lance made of Plum Run flint. Found in Trumbull Co., Ohio, near Mosquito Reservoir. Rob Dills collection. $400.00 – 600.00.

3⅝" two-tone Coshocton Thebes found in Ohio. Rob Dills collection. $1,800.00 – 2,000.00.

3¼" Ohio wide base Dovetail. Made of jem grade Flint Ridge. Rob Dills collection. $800.00 – 1,200.00.

2⅞" Coshocton Dovetail found in Hendricks Co., Indiana. Collection of Rob Horne. $260.00.

HAFTED KNIVES

3 3/16" flint point found in Madison Co., Illinois. Collection of Robert Denother. Personal find.

3 1/16" Dovetail found in Madison Co., Illinois. Collection of Robert Denother. Personal find.

2 5/8" Dovetail found in Madison Co., Illinois. Collection of Robert Denother. Personal find.

2 7/8" Lost Lake found in Madison Co., Illinois. Collection of Robert Denother. Personal find.

4 3/16" Hardin made of Burlington. Found in Madison Co., Illinois. Collection of Robert Denother. Personal find.

3 3/4" Dalton made from Burlington chert. Found in Madison Co., Illinois. Collection of Robert Denother. Personal find.

HAFTED KNIVES

3¼" corner notch knife found in Clarksville, Tennessee. John McCurdy collection. $225.00 – 300.00.

4" Mulberry Creek knife found in Tennessee. John McCurdy collection. $120.00 – 140.00.

3⁹⁄₁₆" long Benton found in Tennessee. John McCurdy collection. $200.00 – 250.00.

3¾" rice lobbed knife found in Gasconade Co., Missouri. Made from mozarkite flint. John McCurdy collection. $100.00 – 135.00.

3⅛" Adena made from Flint Ridge flint. Found in Ashland Co., Ohio. John McCurdy collection. $110.00 – 145.00.

HAFTED KNIVES

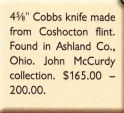

4⅝" Cobbs knife made from Coshocton flint. Found in Ashland Co., Ohio. John McCurdy collection. $165.00 – 200.00.

3⁷⁄₁₆" side notch knife found in Ashland Co., Ohio. John McCurdy collection. $165.00 – 185.00.

4" corner notch knife with one side resharpened down to the notched area. Found in Ashland Co., Ohio. John McCurdy collection. $145.00 – 165.00.

3⅞" Burlington Dalton found in Pike Co., Illinois. Collection of Rick Latell. $650.00.

3⅞" Barbed Hardin made from Burlington. Found in Admas Co., Illinois. Collection of Rick Latell. $850.00.

HAFTED KNIVES

2¾" Barbed Hardin found in Fayette Co., Illinois. Collection of Rick Latell. $350.00.

4¹⁄₁₆" Burlington Dalton found in St. Clair Co., Illinois. Collection of Rick Latell. $350.00.

3¼" Dovetail made from Burlington. Found in Boone Co., Missouri. Collection of Rick Latell. $650.00 – 800.00.

2¹³⁄₁₆" Dalton made from Penters chert. Found in Clay Co., Arkansas. Collection of Rick Latell. $400.00.

3" Edwards chert point found in Coreyll Co., Texas. Collection of Rick Latell. $475.00.

Dalton made from Harvester chert. Found in 1895 in South Co., Missouri. Collection of Rick Latell. $600.00 – 800.00.

HAFTED KNIVES

5½" Adena made from heat-treated Burlington. Found in Osage Co., Missouri. Collection of Rick Latell. $1,800.00.

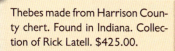

Thebes made from Harrison County chert. Found in Indiana. Collection of Rick Latell. $425.00.

4⅛" Dalton made from purple mozarkite. Found in Pike Co., Illinois. Collection of Rick Latell. $800.00.

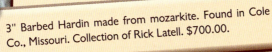

3" Barbed Hardin made from mozarkite. Found in Cole Co., Missouri. Collection of Rick Latell. $700.00.

5¾" Vian Dalton made from Barren Fork chert. Found in Stigler Co., Oklahoma. Found on the Canadian River by a farmer while fishing. Collection of Rick Latell. $3,000.00.

HAFTED KNIVES

4¼" Chesterfield made from Burlington. Found in Cole Co., Missouri. Collection of Rick Latell. Personal find.

3⅞" Agate Basin made from jasper. Found in Colorado. Collection of Rick Latell. $450.00.

3⅛" Scottsbluff made from Boone chert. Found in Mahaska Co., Iowa. Collection of Rick Latell. Not listed.

Holland made from Pitkin. Found in Tennessee downstream from the Olive Branch Site. Collection of Rick Latell. $2,200.00.

Dovetail made from Burlington. Found in Lincoln Co., Missouri. Collection of Rick Latell. $750.00.

HAFTED KNIVES

3⅛" Cody era artifact made from obsidian. Found in Lake View, Oregon. Collection of Ron Van Heukelom. $800.00.

5⅜" Cupp point found in Webster Co., Missouri. Collection of Stephen Burks. $350.00 – 500.00.

3 9/16" black Coshocton notch base Dovetail found in Ohio. Rob Dills collection. $650.00.

5¼" knife found in Greene Co., Missouri. Collection of Stephen Burks. $150.00.

HAFTED KNIVES

4" rice knife found in Stone Co., Missouri. Collection of Stephen Burks. $175.00.

3¼" Adena notched base made from Burlington. Found in Cedar Co., Missouri. Collection of Stephen Burks. $125.00.

4" Burlington artifact found in Greene Co., Missouri. Collection of Stephen Burks. $150.00.

4⅝" Etley made from Burlington. Found in Greene Co., Missouri. Collection of Stephen Burks. $150.00.

4½" Sedalia made from quartzite. Found in St. Clair Co., Missouri. Collection of Stephen Burks. $160.00.

HAFTED KNIVES

5¼" Dalton preform made from Burlington. Found in Greene Co., Missouri. Collection of Stephen Burks. $175.00.

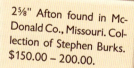

2⅝" Afton made from Reed Springs. Found in Lawrence Co., Missouri. Collection of Stephen Burks. $100.00 – 200.00.

4" Cobbs triangle made from Pitken chert. Found in Crawford Co., Kansas. Collection of Stephen Burks. $200.00.

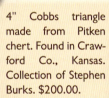

5¾" Etley made from Burlington. Found in Audrain Co., Missouri. Collection of Stephen Burks. $250.00 – 350.00.

2⅝" Afton found in McDonald Co., Missouri. Collection of Stephen Burks. $150.00 – 200.00.

HAFTED KNIVES

2⅝" Afton made from Reed Springs. Found in Barry Co., Missouri. Collection of Stephen Burks. $75.00.

2¾" Hardin found in Stone Co., Missouri. Collection of Stephen Burks. $75.00.

3⅜" Dickson found in Cedar Co., Missouri. Collection of Stephen Burks. $125.00.

5⅜" Neosho knife found in McDonald Co., Missouri. Collection of Stephen Burks. $175.00.

4⅜" Burlington Sedalia found in St. Clair Co., Missouri. Collection of Stephen Burks. $150.00 – 225.00.

4⁷⁄₈" Lerma found in Cherokee Co., Kansas. Collection of Stephen Burks. $200.00 – 300.00.

2³⁄₈" rice side notch made from mozarkite. Found in Wright Co., Missouri. Collection of Stephen Burks. Personal find.

2¼" knife made from mozarkite. Found in Wright Co., Missouri. Collection of Stephen Burks. Personal find.

3³⁄₈" rice side notch made from mozarkite. Found in Laclede Co., Missouri. Collection of Stephen Burks. $150.00.

3" Cupp found in Wright Co., Missouri. Collection of Stephen Burks. Personal find.

HAFTED KNIVES

3½" Burlington Cobbs drill found in Wright Co., Missouri. Collection of Stephen Burks. Personal find.

3⅛" Dalton made from Boyle chert. Found in Kentucky. Collection of Stephen Burks. $350.00.

4⅝" Cobs triangle found in Lawrence Co., Missouri. Collection of Stephen Burks. $200.00 – 300.00.

4½" Burlington Gary found in Greene Co., Missouri. Collection of Stephen Burks. $350.00.

Burlington Etley found in Callaway Co., Missouri. Collection of Stephen Burks. $250.00.

Mozarkite Tablerock found in Webster Co., Missouri. Collection of Stephen Burks. $65.00.

Mozarkite Hemphill Dalton found in Webster Co., Missouri. Collection of Stephen Burks. $150.00.

3⁹⁄₁₆" Dickson made from Burlinton. Collection of Stephen Burks. $150.00.

5½" Cobbs blade made from Kanawha Black flint. Found in Scioto Co., Ohio, in Haverhill. Collection of Steve Valentine. Steve wrote in with this photo, "This large Cobbs was found in Haverhill, Ohio, and was found in the bottom of another hunter's boot print in a very sandy field. I had been waiting for this certain field to be plowed and they finally turned it very deep and then we had two days of steady rain on it to wash it down. I knew it would be washed down really good since it's a very sandy field. When I got there around 11:00 a.m. that morning and stepped into the field I noticed a set of tracks in the field and was ticked that someone had beaten me there already, but they were nowhere is sight. Once I got into the field I noticed that this person had only walked the top of the ridge from one end of the field and back to the other end, so I started going up and down the ridge passing by their prints on each trip. On one certain pass I looked down into one of the boot prints and saw the entire edge of this Cobbs in the bottom of the print. I couldn't believe it when I reached in and pulled this piece out. The only thing I can figure is this Cobbs was just below the surface and when they stepped on it they cocked it sideways and exposed it in the boot print." Personal find.

HAFTED KNIVES

2½" Paleo stemmed lance made from Kanawha black flint. Found in Wheelersburg in Scioto Co., Ohio. Collection of Steve Valentine. Personal find.

3¼" Archaic knife found in Scioto Co., Ohio. Collection of Steve Valentine. Personal find.

2⅜" Carter Cave Dovetail found in Scioto Co., Ohio. Collection of Steve Valentine. Personal find.

3⅜" Archaic stemmed knife made from Carter Cave flint. Found in Lawrence Co., Ohio. Collection of Steve Valentine. Personal find.

3¾" heavy duty found along the Ohio River near Wheelersburg. Collection of Steve Valentine. $100.00.

3⅞" Adena point found in 1983 in Lewis Co., Kentucky. Collection of Steve Valentine. Personal find.

HAFTED KNIVES

3" Flint Ridge Adena Robbins found in Greenup Co., Kentucky. Collection of Steve Valentine. Personal find.

3⅛" stemmed point made from Flint Ridge chalcedony. Found in Scioto Co., Ohio. Collection of Steve Valentine. Personal find.

2¼" Big Sandy made from Flint Ridge nethers. Found near Wheelersburg, Ohio. Collection of Steve Valentine. Personal find.

2¼" Kirk corner notch point made from Coshocton flint. Found in Scioto Co., Ohio. Collection of Steve Valentine. Personal find.

3" Flint Ridge Adena found along the Ohio River near Wheelersburg, Ohio. Collection of Steve Valentine. $150.00 – 200.00.

3¾" Turkeytail found in 1979 in Lawrence Co., Ohio. Collection of Steve Valentine. Personal find.

HAFTED KNIVES

3½" Archaic knife found in Lawrence Co., Ohio. Collection of Steve Valentine. Personal find.

3⅞" Cobbs blade found in Adams Co., Ohio. Collection of Steve Valentine. $150.00 – 200.00.

3½" Lost Lake found in Lawrence Co., Ohio. Collection of Steve Valentine. Personal find.

2½" Thebes found in Greenup Co., Kentucky. Collection of Steve Valentine. Personal find.

3" Lost Lake found in Greenup Co., Kentucky. Collection of Steve Valentine. Personal find.

HAFTED KNIVES

2⅛" Carter Cave Lost Lake found in Lawrence Co., Ohio. Collection of Steve Valentine. Personal find.

2⅝" Thebes e-notch made from Carter Cave flint. Found in Lawrence Co., Ohio. Collection of Steve Valentine. Personal find.

2⅜" Archaic side notch found in Scioto Co., Ohio. Collection of Steve Valentine. Personal find.

2¼" Archaic side notch found in Scioto Co., Ohio. The base looks broken but has been worked that way. Collection of Steve Valentine. Personal find.

2⅞" Adena found in Lewis Co., Kentucky. Collection of Steve Valentine. Personal find.

HAFTED KNIVES

2" Lost Lake found in Scioto Co., Ohio. Collection of Steve Valentine. Personal find.

2¾" Boyle chert Adena found in Lawrence Co., Ohio. Collection of Steve Valentine. Personal find.

2⅜" Thebes found in Haverhill, Ohio. Collection of Steve Valentine. Personal find.

Pair of Adena points found in Tennessee. The largest is 3⅜" Collection of Steve Valentine. $200.00.

Ohio Hopewell made from Flint Ridge moss agate. Collection of Todd Walterspaugh. $350.00.

8" Scottsbluff made from yellow jasper. Most likely from Arkansas. Collection of Todd Walterspaugh. Not listed.

Thebes e-notch made from Burlington chert. Found in Washington Co., Missouri. Collection of Todd Walterspaugh. $800.00.

Dover chert artifacts found in Benton Co., Tennessee. Collection of Todd Walterspaugh. Not listed.

7½" Stanfield blade made from Harrodsburg chert. Found on July 22, 1973, in Bartholomew Co., Indiana. Collection of Todd Walterspaugh. Not listed.

HAFTED KNIVES

Hornstone heavy duty from Kentucky. Collection of Todd Walterspaugh. $125.00.

Hornstone Lost Lake found in Breckenridge Co., Kentucky. Collection of Todd Walterspaugh. $1,100.00.

Burlington Snyder point found in Crawford Co., Michigan. Collection of Todd Walterspaugh. $500.00.

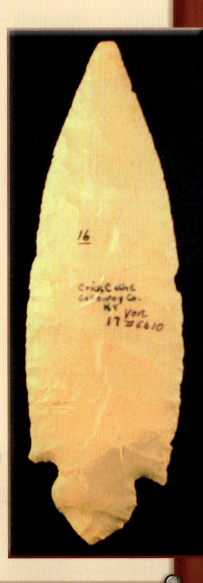

Thebes made from Bayport chert. Found in Lagrange Co., Indiana. Collection of Todd Walterspaugh. $1,000.00.

5½" x 1¾" Turkeytail Fulton from the Crick Cache, investigated by Murray State University. Many blades were found — a lot of them broken (as the case in this one). Collection of William Turner. Unlisted.

HAFTED KNIVES

Flint artifact found in Stoddard Co., Missouri. Collection of Brandon McGowan. Personal find.

Dovetail found in Stoddard Co., Missouri. Collection of Brandon McGowan. Personal find.

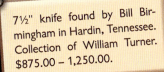

7½" knife found by Bill Birmingham in Hardin, Tennessee. Collection of William Turner. $875.00 – 1,250.00.

Dovetail found in Stoddard Co., Missouri. Collection of Brandon McGowan. Personal find.

Mehlville found in Stoddard Co., Missouri. Collection of Brandon McGowan. Personal find.

2⅞" Lost Lake made from Carter Cave. Found in Carter Co., Kentucky. Collection of Peter Allen. $800.00.

4" Hardin made from Boyles chert. Found in Scott Co., Kentucky. Collection of Peter Allen. $800.00 – 1,200.00.

3½" Eden made from Malhuer chert. Found in Malhuer Co., Oregon, in 2002. Collection of Peter Allen. Personal find.

4¼" Parman from Crump Lake, Oregon. Collection of Peter Allen. Not listed.

HAFTED KNIVES

2¾" Thebes e-notch made from Brassfield chert. Found in Adams Co., Ohio. Collection of Rob Dills. $250.00.

3¾" Scottsbluff made from Edwards. Found in the Sabine River, Lake Toledo Bend, Texas. Collection of Peter Allen. $2,200.00.

Argillite square back knife found in Stokes Co., North Carolina. Collection of Ron L. Harris. Not listed.

Serrated Kirk corner notch found in Lawrence Co., Tennessee. Collection of Ron L. Harris. $375.00.

HAFTED KNIVES

Hardaway Dalton made from green rhyolite. Found in Randolph Co., North Carolina. Collection of Ron L. Harris. $375.00.

Serrated stemmed Kirk made from silicified slate. Found in Forsyth Co., North Carolina. Collection of Ron L. Harris. $125.00.

Serrated stemmed Kirk made from rhyolite. Found in Randolph Co., North Carolina. Collection of Ron L. Harris. $500.00.

Serrated stemmed Kirk made from rhyolite. Found in Catawba Co., North Carolina. Collection of Ron L. Harris. $75.00.

Snowflake rhyolite St. Albans found in Iredell Co., North Carolina. Collection of Ron L. Harris. $250.00.

HAFTED KNIVES

Quartzite Savannah River found in Burke Co., North Carolina. Collection of Ron L. Harris. $250.00.

3¾" Coshocton Meadowood found in Holmes Co., Ohio, near Mt. Hope. Collection of Keith Ray. $200.00 – 250.00.

3³⁄₁₆ Coshocton Dovetail found in Hamilton Co., Ohio. Collection of Keith Ray. $250.00 – 300.00.

Afton made from mozarkite. Found in Webster Co., Missouri. Collection of Richard Eady. $100.00.

HAFTED KNIVES

3⅝" Coshocton Archaic corner notch found in Ohio. Collection of Keith Ray. $150.00 – 200.00.

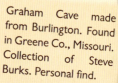

Graham Cave made from Burlington. Found in Greene Co., Missouri. Collection of Steve Burks. Personal find.

2" Big Sandy made from Flint Ridge flint. Found in Ashland Co., Ohio. Author's collection. $40.00 – 60.00.

2¾" Angostura found in Dade Co., Missouri. Collection of Steve Burks. $175.00.

Dalton and Graham Cave. Average size is 1½". All found in Greene Co., Missouri. Collection of Steve Burks. Personal finds.

Knuckolls Dalton made from Reed Springs flint. Found in Greene Co., Missouri. Collection of Steve Burks. Personal find.

7 13/16" Archaic Castroville base tang made of Owl Creek black chert. Found in Bell Co., Texas. Collection of Jack Bates. The material is classic Owl Creek black chert that is found in deposits in Bell and Coryell Co., Texas. $3,000.00.

HAFTED KNIVES

3¾" MacCorkle made of Coshocton flint. Found in Summit Co., Ohio, near the town of Clinton. Collection of Keith Ray. $400.00 – 450.00.

2³⁄₁₆" MacCorkle found in Ohio. Collection of Keith Ray. $125.00 – 150.00.

2¾" MacCorkle made of heavily patinated gray Mercer flint. Found in Mercer Co., Ohio. Collection of Keith Ray. $175.00 – 225.00.

2¼" early Archaic bifurcate made of Coshocton flint. Found in Ross Co., Ohio. Collection of Keith Ray. $125.00 – 150.00.

2⅞" Plains knife found at the Boley site north of Mandan, North Dakota. Collection of Larry Bumann. $90.00 – 150.00.

TANG KNIVES

Knives that were notched so that a cord could be tied around the notched area to keep the knife close at hand during the skinning/butchering process are called tang knives or suspension knives. The notches to create the tang were be placed at the bottom, corner, or side of the knife blade area. Some tang knives may also have been hafted to a handle.

2⅛" mid-back tang knife made of translucent root beer flint. Found in San Marcus, Texas. Collection of Carlos Black. Personal find.

2¼" uniface corner tang knife made from Georgetown. Found in Williamson Co., Texas. Collection of John Selmer. $300.00.

Corner tang knife found in northeast Arkansas near the Arkansas River. Collection of Lyle Guckert. $1,000.00.

Flint artifact found in Red Deer River, Alberta. Collection of Lyle Guckert. Personal find.

TANG KNIVES

Tang knife made from patinated rhyolite. Found in Chatham Co., North Carolina. Collection of Ron L. Harris. Personal find.

Tang knife made from patinated rhyolite. Found in Guilford Co., North Carolina. Collection of Ron L. Harris. $45.00.

Georgia tang or Waller knife. Found in the 1950s in north Georgia. Collection of Ron L. Harris. $75.00.

Tang or Waller knife made from patinated rhyolite. This is a rare find for anywhere in North Carolina since tang or Waller knifes like this are most often found in south Georgia or north Florida. Found in the North Carolina Piedmont Region. Collection of Ron L. Harris. Personal find.

Resharpened Base Tang knife. Found in north Georgia in 1958. Collection of Ron L. Harris. $35.00.

TANG KNIVES

Tang or Waller knife made from Ridge and Valley chert. Found in north Georgia near Rome in 1958. Collection of Ron L. Harris. $125.00.

Tang or Waller knife made from Ridge and Valley chert. Found at an Archaic site near Rome, Georgia, in the 1950s. Collection of Ron L. Harris. $75.00.

Tang or Waller knife made from Fort Payne chert. Found at an Archaic site in northern Georgia in the 1958. Collection of Ron L. Harris. $45.00.

Flint ovoid found in Stoddard Co., Missouri. Collection of Brandon McGowan. Personal find.

BI-POINTED KNIVES

Bi-pointed knives are knives which have points at both ends and were most likely used as a form of hand knife. Many bi-pointed knives are associated with the Woodland period and the Adena culture.

165mm late Prehistoric blade made from high grade basalt. Found on Nightfire Island, California. Collection of Ken Gibson. $450.00.

130mm bi-pointed blade made from obsidian. Found in Fort Rock, Oregon. Collection of Ken Gibson. $500.00.

6½" Prehistoric blade made from obsidian. Found in Spring River, Oregon. Collection of Ken Gibson. $280.00.

280mm bi-pointed blade made from obsidian. Found in Pyramid Lake, Nevada. Collection of Ken Gibson. $900.00 – 1,000.00.

3⅛" bi-pointed blade made from Carter Cave flint. Found in Lawrence Co., Ohio. Collection of Steve Valentine. Personal find.

4⅜" Paleo bi-pointed knife made from Knife River flint. Found in western North Dakota. Collection of Larry Bumann. $250.00.

BI-POINTED KNIVES

2⁵⁄₁₆" flint artifact found in 1992 in Morrow Co., Ohio. Collection of Troy Cuffman. Personal find.

5¼" Adena made from hornstone. Collection of John Selmer. $300.00 – 500.00.

6" Dover Adena blade found in Tennessee. Collection of John Selmer. $400.00 – 600.00.

CRESCENT KNIVES

Crescent knives have been attributed with the Paleo period as well as other time periods and are found in various locations across the country. One side is generally straight to incurvated, while the opposite side curves outward. In some instances, the straight side is "backed," or ground smooth so as not to cut the hand when being held.

Chalcedony Paleo crescent. Found near what would have been the drainage of a pluvial lake bed. Crescents are found in conjunction with Clovis points and are considered part of the Paleo Indian tool kit. It is not known for certain what crescents were used for. Collection of Donald Dix. Personal find.

Coshocton cresent knives. Top two are from Licking Co., Ohio, and the bottom two are from Fairfield Co., Ohio. The largest measures 4". Collection of John Lutz. Not listed.

1¾" Paleo crescent made from brown jasper. Found in Oregon. Collection of John Selmer. $200.00 – 300.00.

46mm crescent made from mottled jasper. Found in the Alvord Desert, Oregon. Collection of Ken Gibson. $350.00.

48mm crescent made from black jasper. Found in the Alvord Desert, Oregon. Collection of Ken Gibson. $250.00 – 300.00.

57mm crescent made from light gray jasper. Found in the Alvord Desert, Oregon. Collection of Ken Gibson. $400.00.

52mm crescent made from honey agate. Found in the Alvord Desert, Oregon. Collection of Ken Gibson. $200.00 – 300.00.

CRESCENT KNIVES

1¾" Agate crescent from the Alvord Desert, Oregon. Collection of Ken Gibson. $250.00.

4⁷⁄₁₆" Paleo uniface crescent knife. Made from Fort Payne and found in Kentucky. Collection of John Selmer. $400.00 – 600.00.

45mm Lunate crescent from Lost River, Oregon. Collection of Ken Gibson. First personal find.

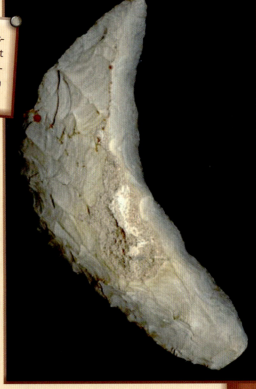

Crescent knife made from Carter Cave. Found in Scioto Co., Ohio. Found on the Gerlach Farm in Franklin Furnace. Collection of Steve Valentine. Personal find.

5½" Crescent knife from the collection of Ron Harris. Not listed.

SQUARE KNIVES

Named for their rectangular shape, square knives have four straight sides and are known to have existed in the Paleo period. This is not a common style, and square knives are very collectible due to the rarity of the style.

4³⁄₁₆" Paleo square knife made from Burlington. Found in Livingston Co., Illinois. Collection of John Selmer. $800.00 – 1,000.00.

3" Upper Mercer Paleo square knife found in Hocking Co., Ohio. Collection of Mike Diano. Personal find.

Square knife found in Webster Co., Missouri. Collection of Stephen Burks. $100.00 – 200.00.

2½" Paleo square knife found in St. Joseph Co., Indiana. Collection of John Selmer. $75.00.

SQUARE KNIVES

3½" Paleo square knife made from Kay County chert. Found in Kay Co., Oklahoma. Collection of John Selmer. $250.00 – 350.00.

3" jasper square knife from Tennessee. Collection of John Selmer. $200.00 – 300.00.

4⁷⁄₁₆" Paleo square knife made from Bisher chert. Found in Fairfield Co., Ohio. Collection of John Selmer. $600.00 – 800.00.

4½" Flint Ridge square knife found in Fairfield Co., Ohio. Collection of Mike Diano. $150.00.

Four Bevel Knives

This strange design is an un-hafted style believed to have been used in hand for skinning animals. Referred to as Harahey knives, they start off as a large bifacially made blade and due to the way they are repeatedly unifacially resharpened, they evolve into a knife with four beveled sides. Harahey knives are very collectible due to the rarity of the style.

3⅞" brown jasper Harahey found in Kansas. Collection of John Selmer. $375.00.

Exhausted Knives

Each time a knife was resharpened, it became smaller in overall size until it reached the point that it either could no longer be resharpened, or became too small for its intended purpose, reaching the point of "exhaustion." In areas where flint was readily available, knives were usually discarded when they began to shrink in size past the point of comfortable use to perform their duties. However, in areas where flint was not readily available, knives were often used down to the point of exhaustion.

2⅛" Scotts Bluff made from Reed Springs and found in Greene Co., Missouri. Collection of Stephen Burks. $275.00.

FOUR BEVEL KNIVES

2⅛" Scotts Bluff found in Webster Co., Missouri. Collection of Stephen Burks. $350.00.

Exhausted knife found in Ohio. Collection of Rob Dills. $5.00 – 8.00.

Exhausted knife found in Ohio. Collection of Rob Dills. $1.00 – 3.00.

Exhausted Big Sandy knife found in Ohio. Authors collection. $25.00 – 35.00.

CHOPPING TOOLS

From cutting wood to splintering bones, chopping tools were as necessary in ancient times as they currently are in modern times. Ancient man used a variety of tools for chopping, most attached to handles, and while the majority were made from hardstone, some were made from flint such as flint axes, celts, and adzes. Just as with their hardstone cousins, flint celts have a straight bit, while flint adzes have a curved bit. Axes made from flint are not grooved as seen on the hardstone varieties, but rather generally notched on two sides.

Celts made from stone are found in most all areas of the county, with a huge selection found east of the Mississippi. A celt, being a simple shaped ungrooved axe with a bit at one end and a poll at the other, was hafted to a wood handle and used for various chopping and bark stripping tasks. Some have speculated that some celts were associated with skinning, but no hard evidence has been proven on this point that I am aware of. When studying the bit end of stone celts, it is common to find very small grooves in the surface from the bit coming up towards the midsection, which strongly suggests it use as a chopping tool.

Celts made from flint are similar in style to their stone celt cousins, and are predominantly percussion flaked. I have seen examples of very flat, well-flaked flint celts that were repaired or resharpened at the bit using large pressure flakes, but that is the only evidence of pressure flaking I have thus come across. Flint celts are usually crudely flaked, which makes the better crafted celts a rare item. Keeping in mind these tools were used for chopping, it is not uncommon to find damage to the bit area.

One thought that I have pondered lately is the specific reason that ancient man crafted celts from flint. I believe that all items were made for a specific reason in ancient times, even though in many cases the exact specific reason remains unknown. Knowing that hardstone and slate celts were the predominant choice for daily use due to the much higher number found when compared to flint celts, and also knowing that flint is more prone to damage than a stone celt, leads one to wonder if flint celts were crafted for a specific task.

Most flint celts that I have handled over the years have been from 2½" to 7" long, with the medium size being 4½" long. As with hoes and spades, larger raw material sections were required for manufacture and thus not every area had a source that would yield such large pieces to work with — so celts are not common finds in all areas. The largest assemblage of flint celts seems to be from the Missouri, Illinois, Indiana area with the most common material being Burlington flint.

Another intriguing thought is that while Dover flint was commonly worked into very large hoes and spades, the number of Dover flint celts is quite low when compared to the number of Burlington celts that were manufactured. Similar to celts in shape are flint adzes. Adzes have a curved bit and were used for woodworking, and were hafted a bit different than celts so that the bit area would be parallel with the surface of the material being worked. Adzes made from flint will often display nice use polish to the bit area.

Flint axes and double bit axes made from flint are not as common as flint celts; however, many were made in ancient times. Often notched at the mid section, it is hard to tell if some axes were actually used for chopping, or if they were used as a variation of the flint hoe and used for cultivation.

FLINT AXES

4⅜" chipped flint axe found in Granville Co., North Carolina. Collection of Frank Loverso. Personal find.

CHOPPING TOOLS

4 1/8" flint axe found in Ohio. Collection of John Lutz. Personal find.

Notched flint celt made from Burlington. Found in Lincoln Co., Missouri. Collection of John Ray. Personal find.

4" flint double bit axe made from Burlington. Found in Greene Co., Missouri. Collection of Stephen Burks. Personal find.

4 3/4" double bit axe found in Greene Co., Missouri. Collection of Steve Burks. $75.00.

CHOPPING TOOLS

Guilford flaked axes made from patinted rhyolite. Found in Randolph, Chatham, and Montgomery Co., North Carolina. Collection of Ron L. Harris. Group $500.00.

169

CHOPPING TOOLS

FLINT CELTS

Group of chipped flint axes. Largest measures 4¼". All found in Wake Co., North Carolina. Collection of Frank Loverso. Personal finds.

Flint celts made of Coshocton. Found in Fairfield Co., Ohio. The largest measures 2½". Collection of John Lutz. $30.00 – 50.00.

Flint celts made from Burlington. The largest measures 3½". Collection of John Lutz. $20.00 – 50.00.

3½" Flint celt found in Perry Co., Ohio. Collection of John Lutz. Personal find.

5½" triangular blade made from Delaware chert. Collection of John Lutz. $100.00 – 200.00.

Selection of flint celts that range in size from 2¼" to 3½" — all from Ohio. $20.00 – 40.00 each.

CHOPPING TOOLS

8¾" flint celt made from Fort Payne chert. Found in Florence, Alabama, in 1978. Collection of John McCurdy. $300.00.

Flint celt made from Burlington. Found in Lincoln Co., Missouri. Collection of John Ray. Personal find.

Flint celt/hoe made from Burlington. Found in Lincoln Co., Missouri. Collection of John Ray. Personal find.

Flint celt made from Burlington. Found in Lincoln Co., Missouri. Collection of John Ray. Personal find.

CHOPPING TOOLS

4 11/16" flint celt made from Burlington. Found in Madison Co., Illinois. Collection of Robert Denother. Personal find.

3 9/16" flint celt found in Madison Co., Illinois. Collection of Robert Denother. Personal find.

3 9/16" flint celt made from Burlington. Found in Madison Co., Illinois. Collection of Robert Denother. Personal find.

2 1/2" flint celt found in Madison Co., Illinois. Collection of Robert Denother. Personal find.

5 1/4" Burlington celt found in Greene Co., Missouri. Collection of Stephen Burks. Personal find.

CHOPPING TOOLS

7" Burlington flint celt found in Webster Co., Missouri. Collection of Stephen Burks. Personal find.

2" to 2¼" flint celts made from Burlington. Found in Webster Co., Missouri. Collection of Stephen Burks. $25.00.

2¼" flint celt or chisel made from Burlington. Found in Webster Co., Missouri. Collection of Stephen Burks. $35.00.

3½" to 4" flint celts made from Mozarkite. Found in Webster Co., Missouri. Collection of Stephen Burks. $50.00.

CHOPPING TOOLS

3" flint celt from southern Illinois. Collection of Steve Colbert. $50.00.

3¾" quartzite flare bit celt. Found Webster Co., Missouri. Collection of Stephen Burks. $75.00.

5" flint celt found in Crittenden Co., Kentucky. Collection of Mike Diano. $75.00 – 100.00.

CHOPPING TOOLS

Flaked flint chisels, celts, and adzes made from patinated rhyolite. Found in Randolph, Chatham, and Montgomery Co., North Carolina. Collection of Ron L. Harris. Group $300.00.

Flaked adz or chisel made from patinated rhyolite. Found in Catawba Co., North Carolina. Collection of Ron L. Harris. $55.00.

4¾" flint celt made from Kanawha black flint. Found in Lawrence Co., Ohio. Collection of Steve Valentine. Personal find.

CHOPPING TOOLS

3⅞" flint celt found in Scioto Co., Ohio. Collection of Steve Valentine. Personal find.

3¾" flint celt made from Kanawha black flint. Found in Scioto Co., Ohio, along Hayport Road in Wheelersburg. Collection of Steve Valentine. Personal find.

3¼" flint celt found in Scioto Co., Ohio. Collection of Steve Valentine. $25.00.

Pair of flint celts found in Lawrence Co., Ohio, about three months apart. Both are made from Carter Cave and the larger of the two measures almost 4". Collection of Steve Valentine. Personal finds.

CHOPPING TOOLS

6¾" flint celt made of Burlington. Found in Missouri. Collection of Kim Radke. $100.00 – 200.00.

FLINT ADZES

4¾" flint adze found in southern Indiana. Collection of Steve Colbert. $250.00.

5½" Burlington adze found in southern Illinois. Collection of Steve Colbert. $250.00 – 300.00.

FARMING AND DIGGING TOOLS

Farming in the area now defined as the continental United States began during the Woodland period, and progressed and grew in importance continually until the point of contact and beyond. When thinking of farming in prehistoric times, images of small patches of maize appear in our minds, but more was cultivated during prehistory than many realize. Maize actually arrived from Mexico around 200 AD, yet it wasn't until around 800 AD that maize became a major food source that developed into large farming and commerce centers such as Cahokia in Illinois. While it was long believed that all agriculture in general followed the trend of importation from Meso American, more recent research and studies have shown that agriculture in prehistoric America actually started much earlier than the arrival of maize, and some species of plants were cultivated from native wild plants, independent of importation from other areas. Maize has a unique trait in that it has more carbon 13 as relative to carbon 12 than other native North American food plants. This difference can be seen when studying the bones of those who ate large quantities of maize after 800 AD, but what about other domesticated foods?

It's interesting to read about the developments over the last 20 years or so in the field of archaeobotany. Archaeobotany is basically the study of plants in prehistoric times. While seeds found in situ can be carbon dated, that simply tells the age of the seed, not if the seed was collected from a wild plant or one that had been domesticated. With the use of SEM (Scanning Electron Microscomerty) seeds can be magnified thousands of times. This allows researchers to study the seed's coat thickness. The thickness of this coating is different on domesticated seeds than on wild seeds, and thus this is one way that researchers can tell if seeds recovered from a site were wild or if they came from cultivated plants.

At the Russell Cave site in Alabama, the charred remains of over 50,000 seeds were found, studied, and determined to be from domesticated chenopodium (also called "goosefoot"), which is a plant native to the area. Carbon dating put the Russell cave seeds into the Early Woodland period at aproxmately 3,000 BC — over 2,000 years before domesticated maize arrived from Mexico. Other indigenous plants that were brought into domestication by native North Americans were marsh elder, squash, sunflower, erect knotweed, little barley, and maygrass. Combined with imported domestic plants that traveled in from Meso America, the native population of ancient North America from the Woodland period on cultivated and harvested such crops as an increasing part of their daily diet.

Some of the largest flint tools made in North America were crafted to assist with moving dirt in one fashion or another. Hoes can range in size from a few inches to well over 15" in length, the larger sized hoes over 10" long are often referred to as spades. The theory that these larger tools were used more for general digging than for direct agriculture use is speculative. There is really no way to know for certain if spades were more task specific than hoes as both often exhibit identical high use polish to the bit areas and are the same in general shape and design. The general difference between the two as seen by collectors is the mere size of the relic. Another factor when determining which term to use is the quality of the flaking. Spades are generally considered to be of higher manufacturing quality.

Flint hoes (and especially spades) were not manufactured in all areas. This is not because hoes were not used as cultivation tools in some locations, but rather because only certain types of flint could be quarried in such a manner to produce large enough slabs to work into such oversized tools. In areas where the manufacture of cultivation tools was not possible with the flint locally available, other materials were used such as wood, bone, horn, and even shell. Shell hoes are commonly found in Florida, and hoes made from moose horn were not uncommon in the northeastern states.

Two types of flint that were widely used for the manufacture of hoes and spades were Dover flint quarried in Stewart Co., Tennessee, and Burlington chert from eastern Iowa. Both of these could be worked into large tools and both had wide distribution areas. I have seen hoes made from Dover flint that were found in Indiana, Illinois, Kentucky, Tennessee, Alabama, and Georgia and Burlington hoes that were recovered in Missouri, Iowa, Illinois, Indiana, and Kentucky. I am certain this is far from a complete list, but will provide the reader with an idea of how far the area of distribution for these two flint types were in ancient times.

Another style of hoe manufactured in ancient times is the notched hoes. Notched hoes are easy to identify with their

FARMING AND DIGGING TOOLS

large notches placed on opposite sides to assist with hafting. Notched hoes are more localized finds, and the majority that I have seen were made from Burlington flint.

While not all hoes will exhibit signs of use polish, the majority of the larger spades and hoes that I have handled do have at least some noticeable polish to the bit area. When used over and over, year after year, the bit area of the hoe would come in contact with the ground hundreds of thousands of times. This repeated contact would polish the flint surface at the bit and the higher flake ridges up to the mid-section of the hoe. One way to tell if damage to the bit end of these tools is recent or ancient is to look for signs of polish where the damage is. If the damaged area is polished over, the damage was ancient and most likely from contact with a stone in the ground while being used. Many of these large tools will have polished over damage area along the bit edge.

HOES AND SPADES

Flint hoe made from Fort Payne chert. Found Yalobusha Co., Mississippi, in the 1960s along the banks of the Yocona River at Enid Lake. Collection of John McCurdy. $700.00.

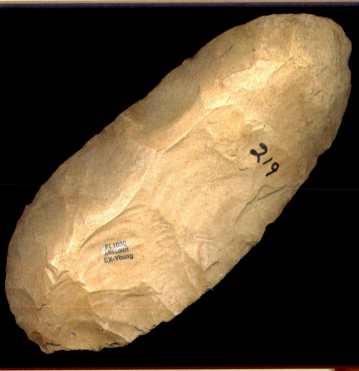

7¾" flint hoe found in Missouri. Collection of Kim Radke. $350.00.

FARMING AND DIGGING TOOLS

4 15/16" double notched hoe found in Illinois. Collection of Musée de la Neufve. Photo by Nicolas Tremblay. $1,000.00.

4 1/4" Burlington hoe found in Webster Co., Missouri. Collection of Stephen Burks. $50.00 – 100.00.

6 1/2" long by 3" chipped hoe found in Fairfield Co., Ohio. The bit does exhibit some use polish. Collection of Mark Morrison. Personal find.

FARMING AND DIGGING TOOLS

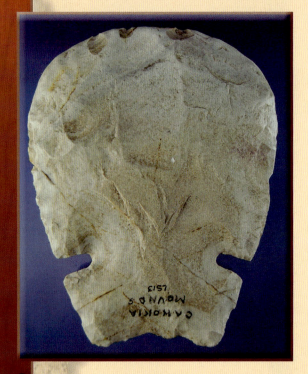

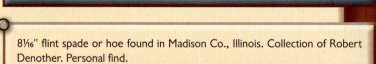

8 1/16" flint spade or hoe found in Madison Co., Illinois. Collection of Robert Denother. Personal find.

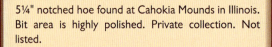

5 1/4" notched hoe found at Cahokia Mounds in Illinois. Bit area is highly polished. Private collection. Not listed.

8 1/16" flint spade or hoe found in Madison Co., Illinois. Collection of Robert Denother. Personal find.

7" x 4 1/2" side notched hoe from Henderson County, Kentucky. Collecton of Jim Crawford — on display at the Museum of Native American Artifacts. Museum quality.

FARMING AND DIGGING TOOLS

A large Midwest spade that measures 13¼" long by 5" wide. Courtesy of the Museum of Native American Artifacts. Museum quality.

Notched hoe from eastern Missouri, 5½" x 4½". Courtesy of the Museum of Native American Artifacts. Museum quality.

Large spade that measures 10¾" long by 4½" wide. Has ancient rechipping on the side of the blade area (most likely done to help with hafting issues). Found in Kentucky. Courtesy of the Museum of Native American Artifacts. Museum quality.

Large hornstone spade that measures 14" by 5¾". Courtesy of the Museum of Native American Artifacts. Museum quality.

FARMING AND DIGGING TOOLS

A very well used spade made from Mill Creek chert that measures 8¾" by 4½". Courtesy of the Museum of Native American Artifacts. Museum quality.

Midwest spade that measures 9 x 3¼". Courtesy of the Museum of Native American Artifacts. Museum quality.

Caddo spade/hoe made of argillite. Measures 9½" x 2¾". From Leflore County, Oklahoma. Courtesy of the Museum of Native American Artifacts. Museum quality.

DIGGERS

Called "flint diggers," "root diggers," and "Sedalia diggers" and more common in the Illinois/Missouri area are tools made from flint that resemble a flint chisel, only with a wider bit area that is not ground or polished. As these tools differ from flint celts in that they are thinner in cross-section and occasionally have minimal pressure flaking on them, the theory has been presented they were used for digging plants and roots.

6¾" Burlington digger found in Jackson Co., Missouri. Collection of Steve Colbert. $200.00 – 250.00.

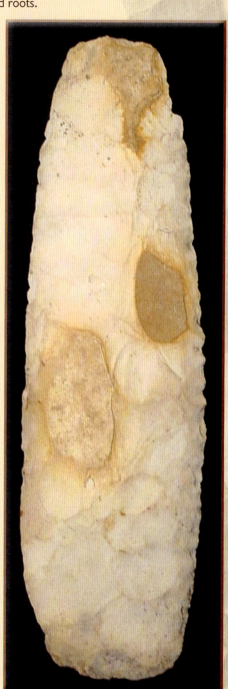

7⅞" Burlington Sedalia digger found in Central Missouri. Collection of Steve Colbert. $250.00 – 300.00.

PERFORATING TOOLS

DRILLS

The task of drilling holes was just as important in ancient times as it is today. Just as we use drill bits that spin and bore, and punches and awls to make holes, so did ancient man. While awls in ancient times were often made from bone with a lesser amount made from flint, drill bits were generally made from flint to complete the tasks of boring holes through bone, wood, and stone.

Drills are associated with all time periods from Paleo on down, with Paleo drills being the most rare. Drills come in many styles, with some designed to be drills from the moment of manufacture, while others were salvaged into drills from larger knives that either broke or were exhausted.

Drills made from flint are unique tools that are easy to identify and fairly common in the artifact marketplace. Ranging from crude hand-held thumb drills to more elaborately flaked notched drills, these tools have always been a favorite to collectors.

There are really three types of drills as far as hafting is concerned although there are many styles as far as basal style goes. The first type of drills are those with expanding bases that were hand held and not hafted to a handle. Smaller expanded base drills are often referred to as thumb drills. The second type of drill are those that have basal styles that imitate point and knife types of the period, many of which may have been (and probably were) worked down from larger knives. The third type of drill was probably never used as a drill, but collectors commonly call them drills and associate them with such a use. They are knives that were worked down by resharpening reductions until they reach the point of exhaustion where they could no longer be used as a viable working knife. This latter group often has the appearance of a drill as it is long and narrow and often the result of repeated unifacial resharpening; however, the majority of the examples I have studied lack any indication that they were in fact used as a functional drills as most do not exhibit drill traits such as use wear, polish, or twist damage to the tip area.

In ancient times, suspension holes were commonly drilled in slate ornaments, wood, and bone handles, and a variety of other items. Even the pottery cultures often drilled suspension holes under or in the rim of some of their pots. This makes sense as the structures that were used in ancient times probably lacked usable shelving — yet plenty of room existed for hanging most anything.

Drills can be as small as sliver sized micro-drills or as large as 6"+ hair pin drills that some speculate may have been used as hair ornamentation. I personally cannot weigh in with an opinion on this use as while I cannot think of a practical reason to have such a long drill that would be prone to breakage, I also have not come across solid documentation in the archaeological record that shows an in situ recovery of such an item around the skull. Whatever their purpose, large, thin drills did exist and were definitely assigned a specific purpose in ancient times.

Nice 4" drill converted from a Dalton knife and made from mozarkite flint. Found in Osage Co., Missouri. Collection of Rick Latall. $200.00 – 300.00.

2" to 4⅞" drills. Various states. Collection of John Selmer. $25.00 – 1,500.00

PERFORATING TOOLS

Some commonly collected styles of drills are:

- T-drills
- expanded base drills
- pin/pencil drills
- notched base drills
- converted knife drills
- converted exhausted knife drills

T-drills

2¾" expanded base drill. Collection of Steve Burks. $65.00.

1¹⁵⁄₁₆" agate drill from New Mexico. Collection of John Selmer. $40.00 – 80.00.

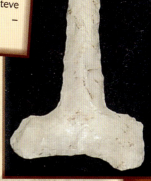

2½" Thebes made from Burlington. Found in Illinois. Collection of Steve Colbert. $200.00 – 250.00.

Expanded Base Drills

Hornstone drill found in Portage Co., Ohio. Jeff Adams collection. Personal find.

Upper Mercer drill found in Portage Co., Ohio. Jeff Adams collection. Personal find.

3¾" drill made from Delaware chert. Found in Lawrence Co., Ohio. Collection of John Lutz. $75.00 – 150.00.

PERFORATING TOOLS

4⅞" Coshocton paddle drill found in Adams Co., Ohio. Collection of John Selmer. $500.00.

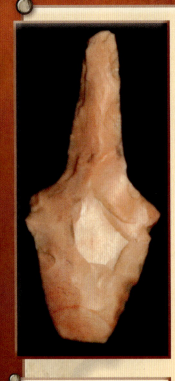

Adena drill. Found in Lincoln Co., Missouri. Collection of John Ray. Personal find.

3⅛" expanded base drill found in Coshocton Co., Ohio. Collection of Keith Ray. $125.00 – 150.00.

3½" Stanfield drill. Collection of John Selmer. $175.00.

1¹⁵⁄₁₆" drill. Found in Madison Co., Illinois. Collection of Mike Denother. Personal find.

PERFORATING TOOLS

3⅛" drill found in Madison Co., Illinois. Collection of Robert Denother. Personal find.

2⅛" drill. Found in Madison Co., Illinois. Collection of Robert Denother. Personal find.

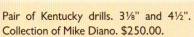

Pair of Kentucky drills. 3⅛" and 4½". Collection of Mike Diano. $250.00.

2¼" drill found in Madison Co., Illinois. Collection of Robert Denother. Personal find.

3¼" drill made from Burlington. Found in Madison Co., Illinois. Collection of Robert Denother. Personal find.

Rhyolite Kirk drill found in Rowan Co., North Carolina. Collection of Ron L. Harris. Not listed.

PERFORATING TOOLS

Rhyolite Kirk corner notch drill. Found in Davie Co., North Carolina. Collection of Ron L. Harris. $75.00 – 125.00.

Set of seven drills from the Hardin Village site located in the Siloam Bottoms of Greenup Co., Kentucky. The largest is around 2". Collection of Steve Valentine. Personal finds.

Group of drills found in Dade Co., Missouri. Collection of Steve Burks. $35.00 – 60.00.

PERFORATING TOOLS

Pin and Pencil Drills

4¼" drill made from Harrison chert. Found in Bartholomew Co., Indiana. Collection of Grady Steele. $450.00.

2¼" drill made from Kanawha black flint. Found in Scioto Co., Ohio. Collection of Steve Valentine. Personal find.

3⅝" Burlington drill found in central Missouri. Collection of Steve Colbert. $200.00 – 250.00.

3¼" drill made from Burlington. Found in Madison Co., Illinois. Collection of Robert Denother. Personal find.

Notched Base Drills

2¼" obsidian drill found in Four Corners, Arizona. Collection of Bruce Fenton. Not listed.

3¾" drill made from river stained Coastal Plains chert. Found in Flint River, Georgia. Collection of Cliff Jackson. $200.00.

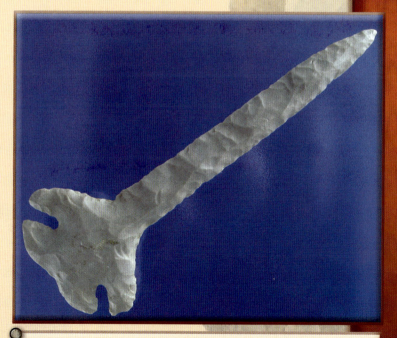

4 1/16" dovetail drill made from hornstone. Found in Evansville, Indiana. Collection of John Selmer. $1,500.00.

PERFORATING TOOLS

3 15/16" fish spear type drill made of Coshocton flint. Found by Jerry Ray in April of 1998 outside of Orrville in Wayne Co., Ohio. Collection of Keith Ray. $275.00 – 350.00.

2 7/16" Drill made from Burlington. Found in Madison Co., Illinois. Collection of Robert Denother. Personal find.

Pair of wing tip drills Found in Scioto Co., Ohio. The left is 2 1/4". Both were found in the same field on the same day in Wheelersburg. Collection of Steve Valentine. Personal finds.

Kirk drill found in Stanly Co., North Carolina. Collection of Ron L. Harris. $225.00.

Speckled rhyolite kirk corner notch drill. Found in Iredell Co., North Carolina. Collection of Ron L. Harris. $100.00 – 200.00.

Rhyolite kirk stemmed drill found in Stanly Co., North Carolina. Collection of Ron L. Harris. $75.00.

Drills Converted from Knives That Were Not Exhausted

Burlington drills found in Callaway Co., Missouri. Collection of Stephen Burks. $60.00 – 150.00.

3¹¹⁄₁₆" paddle drill found in Hamilton Co., Ohio. Collection of Keith Ray. $200.00 – 250.00.

Set of drills made from Burlington. Found in Greene and Stoddard Co., Missouri. Collection of Richard Eady. $50.00 each.

Drills Converted from Exhausted Knives

1⅜" desert drill made from petrified wood. Found in Guadalupe Co., New Mexico. Collection of John Selmer. $75.00.

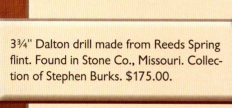

3¾" Dalton drill made from Reeds Spring flint. Found in Stone Co., Missouri. Collection of Stephen Burks. $175.00.

Flint drill found in Stoddard Co., Missouri. Collection of Brandon McGowan. Personal find.

PERFORATING TOOLS

3 7/16" Thebes drill made from Fort Payne. Found in Kentucky. Collection of Grady Steele. $325.00.

4 3/8" Dovetail drill made from Buffalo River chert. Found in the Benton Co., Tennessee, area. Collection of Grady Steele. $350.00.

3 1/8" Dalton drill made from Upper Mercer. Found in Delaware Co., Ohio. Collection of Grady Steele. $275.00.

3 3/4" Dovetail drill made from Hornstone. Found in Garrard Co., Kentucky. Collection of Grady Steele. $450.00.

3 9/16" Pinetree drill made from Buffalo River chert. Found in Decatur Co., Tennessee. Collection of Grady Steele. $500.00.

PERFORATING TOOLS

3⅝" drill made from Flint Ridge flint. Found in Carroll Co., Kentucky. Collection of Grady Steele. $700.00.

3⅝" rare style Decatur made from hornstone. Found in Cumberland Co., Tennessee. This knife is near to the point of exhaustion as far as use for cutting goes, and would have been a potential candidate for conversion to a drill with a few more resharpenings. Collection of Grady Steele. $1,200.00.

Rhyolite paddle drill found in Montgomery Co., North Carolina. Collection of Ron L. Harris. Not listed.

Dalton drill found in Perry Co., Illinois. Collection of Jason Dunihoo. Personal find.

PERFORATING TOOLS

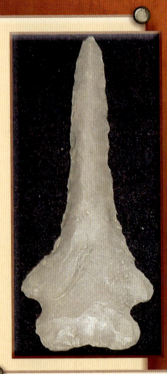

2⅞" Coshocton drill found north of Columbus, Ohio. Collection of Keith Ray. $75.00 –100.00.

2⅝" Hardin made from Burlington. Found in Missouri. Collection of Steve Colbert. $250.00 – 350.00.

3⅜" drill made from hornstone. Found in Kentucky. Collection of Steve Colbert. $250.00 – 300.00.

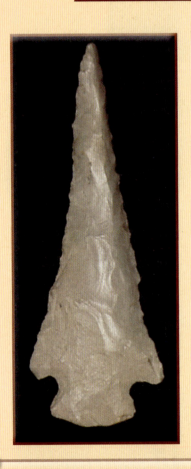

Hornstone Dovetail found in Kentucky. Collection of Steve Colbert. $350.00 – 450.00.

4¼" Lost Lake made of Carter Cave. Found in Barren Co., Kentucky. Collection of Steve Colbert. $500.00 – 600.00.

Hornstone Adena. Found in Turner Creek in Montgomery Co., Illinois. Collection of Steve Colbert. $350.00 – 400.00.

PERFORATING TOOLS

AWLS, REAMERS, AND PERFORATORS

In addition to drills that were spun to create a hole, several other tools known as awls, reamers, and perforators were used in ancient times to punch holes direct through softer material such as leather and skins with the use of direct hand pressure.

Awls and reamers are basically one in the same and often were made to fit easily in hand with a slight bend or curve to them. While they can look very similar to drills, their base or bottom was not made to be hafted into a handle or shaft.

Perforators are easily identifiable by a short protrusion at the top of the tip area. This type of tool was made from flakes as well as being salvaged from broken or exhausted flint points or small knives.

Awls

Examples of awls found in Ashland Co., Ohio. Author's collection. $1.00 – 5.00.

Perforators

2 11/16" Folsom perforator/graver tool found in Kings Co., California. Collection of John Selmer. $750.00. (Value reflects rarity of point style.)

Pair of ¾" perforators found in Scioto Co., Ohio. The top example is made from Zaleski and the bottom from Carter Cave. Collection of Steve Valentine. Personal finds.

WOODWORKING TOOLS

From knife handles to dart foreshafts to spear and arrow shafts to canoes, ancient man had a variety of tools he created for the purpose of working wood. Chisels and gouges were made to work larger sections of wood into the various items used by ancient man while spokeshaves and shaft scrapers were made to work smaller thinner sections into arrow, dart, and spear shafts.

FLINT CHISELS

One of my favorite tool forms is the chisel. I think as collectors, we tend to focus on the raw materials that we are accustomed to seeing in the marketplace — those being items made from flint, slate, stone, bone, and shell. Since most all of the items crafted from wood have long since rotted away, we tend not to think of wooden artifacts as their existence in modern times is rare. However, wood was an easily obtainable and easily worked natural resource for ancient man. The recovery of stone, slate, antler, bone, and flint chisels easily leads one to conclude that woodworking in ancient times was not a rare occurrence.

Chisels made from flint vary from semi-crudely fashioned to very well made. All are thin in width and thicker in cross-section and made from percussion flaking. Most have a nicely ground bit with some examples exhibiting use polish. I have found the bit area averages around 1" wide and the overall length can be from 3" to 7" long. There is seldom any poll damage which leads me to believe that these were in fact hand-held tools and not hafted as has been suggested in some of the older publications.

Set of three flint chisels found in Ashland, Kentucky. Collection of John Lutz. $30.00 – 80.00 each.

6" Burlington chisel found in central Illinois. Collection of Steve Colbert. $350.00 – 400.00.

Highly polished flint chisel found in Arkansas. Collection of John Lutz. $200.00 – 300.00.

4½" creek stained Burlington Chisel found in western Kentucky. Collection of Steve Colbert. $250.00 – 300.00.

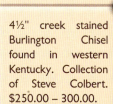

3¼" Mozarkite gouge found in Laclede Co., Missouri. Collection of Stephen Burks. $25.00 – 50.00.

WOODWORKING TOOLS

Small 1½" flint chisel found in Ashland Co., Ohio. Author's collection. $10.00 – 20.00.

4" flint chisel made from Kanawha flint. Found on the Goldcamp site in Lawrence Co., Ohio, on 6/4/09. Collection of Steve Valentine. Personal find.

4" flint chisel made from Kanawha flint. Found on the Goldcamp site in Lawrence Co., Ohio, on 6/3/09. Collection of Steve Valentine. Personal find.

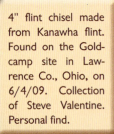

1¾" flint chisel found in Ashland Co., Ohio. Author's collection. $10.00.

2¾" chisel found in North Carolina. Author's collection. $10.00 – 15.00.

SPOKESHAVES AND SHAFT SCRAPERS

The terms "spokeshave" and "shaft scraper" are both terms that describe tools used to scrape and shape wooden arrow and spear shafts. By drawing this tool down a section of sapling or cane, it would remove bark and thin thicker sections to make a uniform shaft.

Examples of Hand-held Spokeshaves

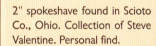

3⅝" Paleo uniface tool with spokeshave. Found in Ohio. Collection of John Selmer. $250.00.

2" spokeshave found in Scioto Co., Ohio. Collection of Steve Valentine. Personal find.

Hand-held spokeshave found in Ohio. Collection of Rob Dills. $10.00 – 25.00.

WOODWORKING TOOLS

4½" hand-held spokeshave found in Colorado. Author's collection. $30.00 – 50.00.

Examples of Knife Forms That Double as Spokeshaves

3 1/16" kays with spokeshave. Made from Horse Creek chert and found in Indian Creek, Missouri. Collection of John Selmer. $200.00.

Ohio corner notch knife (micro-notch style) with a nice spokeshave in one blade edge. John Lutz collection. $50.00 – 75.00.

3 9/16" Paleo combination tool made from Coshocton flint. Found in New London, Ohio. Collection of John Selmer. $75.00.

Spokeshave blade found in Ashe Co., North Carolina. Collection of Ron L. Harris. $65.00.

Archaic blade found in Pittsfield, Massachusetts, along the Housatonic River. Spokeshave in one side. Collection of Bruce Fenton. $40.00.

Exhausted Big Sandy knife from Ohio that was used as a knife until the point of exhaustion. The ancient owner then placed a spokeshave in the side of one blade edge to convert it to a different usable tool form. $20.00 – 40.00.

Woodworking Tools

Hafted shaft scrapers were not coverted from knives, but rather were intentionally made for the sole purpose of be hafted to a handle and used to scrape shafts.

Examples of Shaft Scrapers

Shaft scraper found in Licking Co., Ohio. Collection of John Lutz. $50.00 – 100.00.

Edgefield type hafted shaft scraper made from patinated rhyolite. Found in Wilkes Co., North Carolina. Collection of Ron L. Harris. $35.00.

3" spokeshave from Ohio. Collection of Steve Valentine. Not listed.

2¼" spokeshave found in Scioto Co., Ohio. Made on a uniface flake. Very nice sharp cutting edge on the inside edge of the piece. Collection of Steve Valentine. Personal find.

3" spokeshave found in Scioto Co., Ohio. Collection of Steve Valentine. Personal find.

WOODWORKING TOOLS

Nice selection of hafted shaft scrapers found in Ohio. Collection of Rob Dills. Values range from $35.00 – 140.00.

3" hafted shaft scraper found in south Georgia. Made from an exhausted knife. Author's collection. $15.00 – 25.00.

2¾" hafted shaft scraper found in south Georgia. Made from an exhausted knife. Author's collection. $15.00 – 25.00.

2½" hafted shaft scraper found in south Georgia. Made from an exhausted knife. Author's collection. $15.00 – 25.00.

SCRAPERS

Scrapers from various counties in North Carolina. Collection of Frank Loverso. Personal finds.

One of the most common artifact types found around any area of ancient occupation are scrapers. Used to scrape hides as well as other similar tasks, scrapers come in a variety of styles. Some scrapers were made specifically from raw material to be scrapers, while others were salvaged from broken or damaged points and knives.

While many scrapers were made from flakes of flint and designed to be held in hand, others were hafted to a handle and often made from damaged or exhausted knives. The thumb scrapers were small scrapers made specifically to fit comfortably in one's hand. Edge scrapers, which are hand-held uniface scraping tools, were made from sections of flint that were left over from manufacturing other flint knives and tools. In some areas, large "turtle-back" scrapers are found. This type is very thick and often exceeds 3" in length.

The presence of a multitude of scrapers found in a field is a good indication of occupation in that area.

Shown here are two Hopewell artifacts. On the left is a Hopewell knife, while the artifact on the right is a hafted scraper salvaged from an exhausted knife. Judging by the width of the bases, these relics both started out as similar sized knives. Collection of Jeff Adams.

SCRAPERS

HAFTED SCRAPERS

Group of hafted scrapers found in Fairfield Co., Ohio. Collection of John Lutz. Not listed.

Savannah River hafted scraper made from rhyolite. Found in Catawba Co., North Carolina, in the 1960s near the Catawba River. Collection of Ron L. Harris. Personal find.

SCRAPERS

Frame of hafted scrapers from various locations and made of various materials. Collection of Kirk A. Haas. $2.00 – 40.00 ea.

Nice selection of assorted hafted scrapers found in Ohio. Collection of Lisa Goins. $3.00 – 10.00.

Nice selection of assorted hafted scrapers found in Ohio. Collection of Lisa Goins. $3.00 – 10.00.

SCRAPERS

2" Archaic bevel scraper made from Flint Ridge. Found in Licking Co., Ohio. Collection of Mike Diano. Not listed.

2" Thebes hafted scraper found in Scioto Co., Ohio. Collection of Steve Valentine. Personal find.

Flint artifact found in Stoddard Co., Missouri. Collection of Brandon McGowan. Personal find.

THUMB SCRAPERS

Thumbscrapers found in Ohio. Lisa Goins collection. $ .50 – 3.00.

SCRAPERS

Assortment of Ohio thumb-scrapers. Lisa Goins collection. $.50 – 3.00.

HAND SCRAPERS

Flint scrapers found in Webster Co., Missouri. Collection of Stephen Burks. $5.00 – 20.00.

2½" to 2⅝" Burlington scrapers found in Webster Co., Missouri. Collection of Stephen Burks. $5.00 – 15.00 each.

SCRAPERS

2⅝" Burlington round knife scraper found in Webster Co., Missouri. Collection of Stephen Burks. $30.00 – 50.00.

Silicified slate scraper found in Catawba Co., North Carolina, near Terrell. Collection of Ron L. Harris. $10.00 – 20.00.

GOUGE TIP BLUNTS

Occasionally seen are what looks to be hafted scrapers, but these were possibly used for a different task altogether. These anomalies are not quite as rounded on their tops as scrapers are, with their tips often being more straight across than rounded. The flaking to the tip area is done in such a way as to leave the center surface scooped out as is seen on various other gouge style tools. The two examples shown here were found in Ohio and are from the Lisa Goins collection.

MISCELLANEOUS FLINT ARTIFACTS

In addition to projectile points, knives, and tools, collectors often run into a few other styles of flint artifacts that really do not fit into the artifact categories previously discussed, yet they are still artifacts and worthy of mention and review.

ECCENTRICS

When it comes to items of intrigue made in prehistoric times, eccentrics top the list. Knapped pieces of flint intentionally made into bizarre styles with strange shapes and often with multiple notched areas, the purpose of eccentrics remains a mystery. The most plausible theory to me is that eccentrics were simply practice pieces for young knappers who were being taught the art of flint knapping. How better for a grandfather to show a grandson how to notch a point than to take a piece of flint and put some notches in it while explaining the technique, then handing that piece of flint to the youngster to try his hand at it. Eccentrics have been found in all areas, and remain very collectible to those of us who enjoy oddities.

29mm obsidian eccentric from Valley Falls, Oregon. Collection of Ken Gibson. $25.00.

1¼" eccentric made of agate. Found in Sioux Co., North Dakota. Collection of Larry Bumann. Not listed.

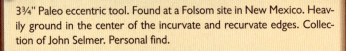

3¾" Paleo eccentric tool. Found at a Folsom site in New Mexico. Heavily ground in the center of the incurvate and recurvate edges. Collection of John Selmer. Personal find.

3⅛" flint eccentric. Found caught in the exposed roots of a tree along the eroded shore of a local lake in Barry Co., Missouri. Collection of Mike Menichetti. Personal find.

⅞" eccentric. Found in Chavez Co., New Mexico. Collection of John Selmer. $100.00.

MISCELLANEOUS FLINT ARTIFACTS

CORES

One of the first steps in manufacturing an item from flint is to reduce a larger piece of material into smaller more manageable sections. Dividing this large piece by fracturing sections from the outside would leave a center section called a "core." Flint cores can be found at most quarry sites, as well as many camp areas.

Collection of flint cores. The largest is 1¾". All found in Fairfield Co., Ohio, on the Cupp site. Collection of John Lutz. $10.00 – 50.00.

Flint Ridge cores from Fairfield Co., Ohio. Collection of John Lutz. Personal finds.

Flint Ridge cores from Fairfield Co., Ohio. Collection of John Lutz. Personal finds.

Beautiful Flint Ridge flint core found in Ohio. John Lutz collection. $80.00 – 100.00 based on rare blue color.

MISCELLANEOUS FLINT ARTIFACTS

Pair of Flint Ridge flint cores found in Ohio. Collection of John Lutz. $35.00 – 45.00.

Assortment of Flint Ridge flint cores found in Ohio. Collection of John Lutz. $10.00 – 100.00.

LANCETS AND BLADELETS

These small flake cutting tools are often found on Hopewell sites and were most likely attached to a slotted section of wood or bone in a row to create a cutting edge.

Flint Ridge Hopewell bladelets found in Poertage Co., Ohio. Jeff Adams collection. $1.00 – 3.00.

Flint Ridge bladelets/core shop material found in Fairfield Co., Ohio. Collection of John Lutz. $1.00 – 3.00.

Flint Ridge bladelets found in Fairfield Co., Ohio. Largest measures 1¾". Collection of John Lutz. $1.00 – 3.00.

MISCELLANEOUS FLINT ARTIFACTS

FLINT SAWS

Used for heavy cutting jobs, the serrations on flint saws are generally larger and wider spaced than on most knife forms. Flint saws we most often crafted from large flakes and hand held.

2 1/16" uniface knife made from Coastal Plains chert. Found in Alabama. Collection of John Selmer. $40.00 – 60.00.

Burlington flake saw blade found in Greene Co., Missouri. Collection of Stephen Burks. Personal find.

4 5/8" Carter Cave Archaic saw found in southeastern Kentucky. Collection of John Selmer. $400.00.

MULTI-PURPOSE TOOLS

Some great examples of flint tools can be found where ancient man created one tool that would serve multiple uses. Knifes, scrapers, spokeshaves, and gravers were often combined into one tool.

3" multi-purpose scraper knife made of mozarkite. Found in Webster Co., Missouri. Collection of Stephen Burks. $50.00 – 75.00.

MISCELLANEOUS FLINT ARTIFACTS

Graver

Knife Edge

Spokeshave

Chisel/Gouge

Found in Colorado, this multi-purpose tool is like a prehistoric "Swiss army knife." With a knife edge, chisel end, spokeshave, and a graver spur, this would be the perfect tool for making foreshafts and knife handles. Author's collection. $100.00 – 150.00.

FLINT HAMMERSTONES AND KNAPPING STONES

Hammerstones were used in the manufacture of flint tool as well as stone tools. In the case of stone tool manufacture, hammerstones were generally made of hardstone and held in hand or grooved and hafted and struck against the stone item being shaped to peck the surface. In the manufacture of flint items, hammerstone made from flint (generally called flint knapping stones) were used in the percussion flaking process. Hammerstones are round in shape and have one or two ends that are rough in appearance and exhibit small nicks, chips, and dings from use. Hammerstone values range from less than $1.00 to $5.00.

Flint hammerstones found in Fairfield Co., Ohio. Largest measures 2". Collection of John Lutz. Personal finds.

1¼" flint hammerstone found in Ashland Co., Ohio. Author's collection. $2.00.

Two flint hammerstones found in Ohio. The close-up view shows the rough appearance of the surface from repeated use. Collection of Keith Ray. $1.00 – 5.00.

MISCELLANEOUS FLINT ARTIFACTS

CACHES AND CACHE BLADES

When a group of artifacts are found together, it is referred to as a "cache." Caches of preforms as well as completed points, knives, and other tool types have been found in most every area. Caches can range from a couple artifacts to thousands.

Pictured here are some nice caches that have been kept together.

Cache of blades/preforms made from Kanawha. Found around the northeast Ohio/ Pennsylvania border. The largest is 6". Collection of John Lutz. $3.00 – 5.00.

Cache of pickwicks found together in Robertson Co., Tennessee, by Jim Loughman in April 1996. Collection of Jim & Nancy Loughman. Personal finds.

Adena cache made from Bayport chert. Found in Bay Co., Michigan, in the 1960s. Collection of Todd Walterspaugh. Not listed.

219

MISCELLANEOUS FLINT ARTIFACTS

3⅞" to 4⅞" cache of blades. All made from rhyolite. Found in Alleghany Co., North Carolina. Collection of John Selmer. $400.00.

4½" North cache blade made from heat-treated Burlington. Found in Fulton Co., Indiana. Collection of John Selmer. $375.00.

4" cache blade from from Upper Mercer. Found in Perry Co., Ohio. Collection of Mike Diano. $250.00.

MISCELLANEOUS FLINT ARTIFACTS

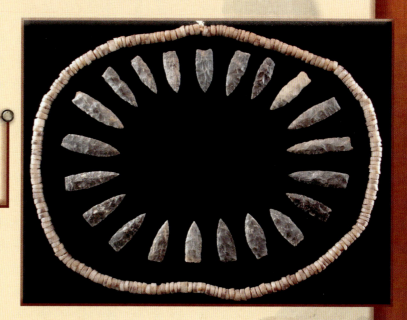

Guntersville "quiver" point cache made from Ridge and Valley chert. Found in Monroe Co., east Tennessee, along the Tellico River near Tellico Plains. Collection of Ron L. Harris. $500.00.

Cache of 21 rhyolite blades and a large scraper. Field found in Catawba Co., North Carolina, in the mid 1950s. The site is near the old Sulphur Springs Resort that is now the Catawba Springs Golf Community. Collection of Ron L. Harris. $500.00 – 800.00.

MISCELLANEOUS FLINT ARTIFACTS

Banded rhyolite cache blades found in Davie Co., North Carolina. This cache of 348 blades was found in the spring of 1955 at a site along the South Yadkin River. The wooded area was being cleared for development. Collection of Ron L. Harris. $3,500.00.

MISCELLANEOUS FLINT ARTIFACTS

348 CACHE BLADES – SOUTH YADKIN RIVER – DAVIE CO., N. C.
ONE OF LARGEST FLINT CACHES EVER DISCOVERED IN NORTH CAROLINA

MISCELLANEOUS FLINT ARTIFACTS

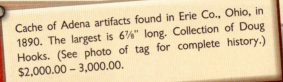

Cache of Adena artifacts found in Erie Co., Ohio, in 1890. The largest is 6⅞" long. Collection of Doug Hooks. (See photo of tag for complete history.) $2,000.00 – 3,000.00.

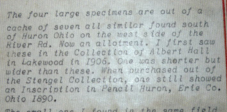

The four large specimens are out of a cache of seven all similar found south of Huron Ohio on the west side of the River Rd. Now an allotment. I first saw these in the Collection of Albert Hall in Lakewood in 1906. One was shorter but wider than these. When purchased out of the Stengel Collection, one still showed an Inscription in Pencil Huron, Erie Co. Ohio 1890.

The small one I found in the same field at the west end.

Three blade cache found in Coshocton Co., Ohio. The largest is 3⅝" long. Collection of Doug Hooks. $800.00 –1,200.00.

Cache of seven blades found in Coshocton Co., Ohio. The largest measures 3½" long. This is part of an original cache of over 100 blades. Collection of Doug Hooks. $2,000.00 – 3,000.00.

MISCELLANEOUS FLINT ARTIFACTS

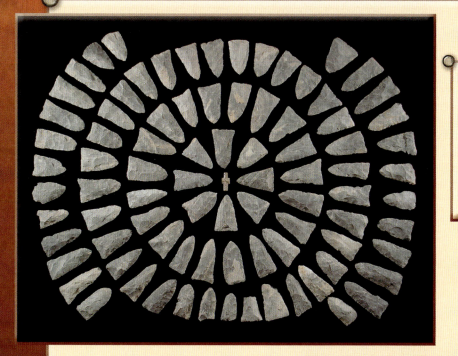

Banded rhyolite cache blades found in Patrick Co., Virginia. This cache of 85 blades was discovered near Ararat in 1963 during farming operations. The nearest source for this rhyolite material is the Uwharrie Mountain range in south-central North Carolina near Albemarle. The staurolite cross in the center was found in Patrick County, Virginia, but was not associated with the blade cache. Collection of Ron L. Harris. $3,000.00.

Rhyolite cache found in Iredell Co., North Carolina. Discovered while breaking new ground for farming operations in May of 1980 on a farm near the Scotts community. The cache consists of 41 rhyolite blades, points, and knives in addition to a crystal graver, a Wade Point (type and material foreign to area), and a banded slate elongated fan-tail birdstone with eye stalks. The birdstone is undrilled and was damaged. There are slight tally marks on the ridge of the back. This was a very unusual find for North Carolina. Collection of Ron L. Harris. $2,500.00.

3½" to 4" Etley cache found in Tunnel Cave in Pulaski Co., Missouri. Collection of Richard Eady. $400.00 – 600.00.

The Tusc River Cache

In addition to writing books on artifacts, I own several artifact-related websites as well as my main business which is doing artifact authentication and an artifact auction company where we auction collections of artifacts from all over the United States. Between all of the above, a lot of phone calls and emails come in from people wanting to sell or auction their artifacts. Some are just single pieces, while others are larger collections, and many are just people looking for information on what they have. One email that came in caught my interest as it was about a family farm collection from here in Ohio, and it was only a couple hours drive south of me. In the photos was a nice selection of field grade points, some tools, a few decent flint knives, and a few Adena blades. I contacted the owner and she stated there were some other items not photographed, and by the end of the conversation we set a day and time for me to take a hands-on look at the collection. I always enjoy looking over and studying field found collections, even if a deal could not be struck so I called my good friend Doug Hooks and off we went down to Tuscarawas County to look at the collection.

After arriving and meeting the family, Doug and I sat at the kitchen table with cups of fresh coffee and began sorting through a couple trays of common and broken points, some nicer knives, and an assortment of scrapers — the type of assemblage you would expect from a farm collection. What we didn't expect was the several trays the owner brought out next. Carefully placed on towels in the tray was a nice selection of Flint Ridge flint Adena cache blades, several layers deep. The owner recounted how and where her father retrieved the pieces along the edge of a field that borders the Tuscarawas River. Doug and I discussed the collection, and agreed to partner up on the purchase of the collection and display it for a year or so and then split the proceeds if and when we sold it. The deal done, we loaded the relics into the car and headed out for the two hour drive home. We talked about the cache all the way, and by the time we reached my farm that night, I could tell that Doug had fallen in love with the cache, and we both agreed it should not be split up and sold individually. Within a few days, Doug had talked me out of my ownership share, with the promise that I could visit it whenever I wanted to.

Included in the cache were over 100 Flint Ridge blades, around 75% which were complete. The largest blade is 7⅛" long.

Part of a 100+ piece cache recovered by Eugene Schlupp on his farm along the Tuscarawas River in Tuscarawas Co., Ohio. Doug Hooks collection.

MISCELLANEOUS FLINT ARTIFACTS

The Bates Cache – Reunited!
Story submitted by Brad Simmerman

This cache of six big blades shown here was plowed up by a farmer named Lynn Bates in Garvin Co Oklahoma, near the town of Stratford and the South Canadian River. Stratford is only a few miles from where the late authenticator Greg Perino resided, and Mr. Perino bought this cache from Lynn, and then proceeded to try to find a buyer for it. Mr. Perino wrote to Mr. Paul Saunders of Virginia and inquired as to whether he would be interested in the group, which he said were made from "a good grade of Stringtown Flint" and that they were probably Calf Creek preforms. I still have the original letter Mr. Perino mailed to Mr. Saunders.

The blades in this cache are 5¼" to 7" long and 2½" – 3⅝" wide. They are pictured in WW #10, pgs 107 and 109. Provenance to the finder goes as follows: Found by and ex Collection of Lynn Bates, ex Greg Perino, ex Paul Saunders, ex Rick Fitzgerald, ex Todd Walterspaugh (4), and ex Paul Saunders (2). Brad Simmerman, is the current collector of all six blades.

I first saw the Bates cache offered for sale on eBay in late 2004. I had recently become interested in Native American artifacts and had just begun collecting. As I was in the middle of five surgeries to correct a back injury I had received at work, I had plenty of time to look online. The person selling the cache was a gentleman named Todd Walterspaugh who I had met online recently. Todd and I had become friends in a short period of time as he helped me learn about reproductions and how to become a collector of authentic artifacts.

I emailed Todd and told him I thought the cache was beautiful, but they were unfortunately out of my price range. I was not yet buying higher quality pieces, but that sure didn't stop me from admiring them. Todd informed me that he had an original letter from Mr. Perino and that he had bought the four pieces at auction. I asked about the other two pieces to the cache, and he said he had no idea as to their whereabouts, but they had not been sold during the auction. The cache went unsold on eBay, and a few weeks later I told Todd if it was me, I would put them in a frame and keep them forever. I was already a huge fan of the work Mr. Perino had done, and I was convinced this was a one of a kind thing that should be cherished. Todd agreed and they were never again offered for sale.

I was lucky enough to see the cache a couple of times in person. The first time was at the Collinsville Show in 2005 when Todd brought them along just to show me and they were more beautiful in person than the pictures I had seen. This was also the first time my son and I had met Todd in person. I saw the cache again in June of that same year, when my son, Bill, and I met Todd at his home in Galesburg, Michigan. Todd had invited us up for the NASCAR race at Michigan International Speedway. While we had met face to face for only a few minutes at the Collinsville show, we had become good friends through our emails and artifact dealings. The Walterspaugh family opened their home and their hearts to us, and it was a race weekend I will never forget. In the back of my mind, I held out hope that one day I just might be able to buy these four out of six pieces from the Bates Cache from Todd.

As the years passed, Todd and I became close friends. Finally, in 2008, I received a settlement for my back injury, and the first thing I did was ask Todd if he would consider selling me the cache. He answered that I was the one who talked him into keeping them — yet after some time, lots of talk, and negotiations, a deal was reached and I took possession of The Bates Cache at the Collinsville Show, Saturday March 8, 2008. Almost immediately after I got home, I tried to contact any people who had been involved with the cache along the way. I talked to Rick Fitzgerald of Oklahoma as the cache was pictured as being in his collection in Who's Who #10. Mr. Fitzgerald informed me that he had no idea of the whereabouts of the other two blades, but that I should ask the owner of the auction company that sold the blades to Todd. I contacted the auction house owner, and he told me that a "reclusive Florida collector" had bought the cache, but if he ever heard they were for sale he would let me know. At that point, I resigned myself to the fact that I would probably never see the other two blades, much less be able to acquire them and reunite the entire cache.

A year later, in March of 2009 Todd visited at my home for a week and we spent four days hunting the fields and creeks of west central Missouri searching for artifacts and really enjoying our time together. The Collinsville Artifact Show was scheduled for March 7 – 8, so on Friday March 6 we headed east. After a short stop at Graham Cave State Park we continued the journey and arrived at Collinsville in plenty of time for Todd to set up. Saturday found me going from room to room visiting with people I had met and become friends with through artifact collecting. Before I could believe it, the day was over and it was time for the Central States Meeting to begin. After dinner and a restless night, I met Todd at the show early, and I decided I needed to make one trip around the whole show room to really look at everything. I picked a direction and took off walking. As I started down the first aisle, I stopped and chatted with various collectors and dealers and then ventured across the aisle and began to look at the displays there. The artifacts were mainly from the southeast area of the country and I was admiring some beautiful pieces when I noticed two large blades and a 3x5 index card with the following words written on it... "Lynn Bates Cache – 2 of 6 Preforms Found Near Stratford, OK - Calf Creek Preforms."

I could not believe my eyes! I let out a whoop and the gentleman behind the table was a bit surprised and said, "Excuse me?" I apologized, then informed him that I was the present owner of the other four blades from the cache. His eyes lit up and he got very excited and we shook hands and began talking about the cache. It turns out this was Paul Saunders, the man who had originally purchased the entire cache from Mr. Perino. He said he purchased them in 1993, but that he was unsure exactly when they had been found. We then went through how he had sold them and how I had acquired the other four blades. Finally I asked if he would be willing to sell me his two, so I could reunite the cache and a deal was reached. I left the two blades laying there on his table as I had to show them to Todd "in-situ" so to speak, Todd had two tables, so he was reluctant to leave, but he could tell there was something special happening by my excitement, so he got the neighboring people to agree to watch his display. When we got back to Paul's tables, I just stood there and let Todd find the blades himself, he finally saw the blades and card, and you should have seen the size of his eyes! As it turns out, Todd had bought two points from Paul the day before, but had somehow missed seeing the big blades and the index card with the cache information. I am still not sure who was the most excited at this point, Todd or myself — all I knew was that the Bates cache would soon be reunited in one frame, and if I had anything to do with it they would never be separated again. I immediately went and bought a beautiful frame from Jim Cox that would hold the cache and some of the paperwork that pertained to it. It was truly a day to remember, and it topped off a week spent with a friend that I will never forget.

AUTHENTICITY ISSUES

While collecting ancient artifacts is a truly rewarding hobby, it also has its pitfalls. As with any collecting field, artifact collecting has its share of dubious reproductions and modernly altered items. The problem that arises with flint artifacts is two-fold: items that are complete reproductions made in modern times and items that are authentic artifacts, but have a damaged area that was corrected by modern rechipping. In both cases, the optimum value of the item is seriously compromised. The more perfect and beautiful an artifact is, the higher the chance that it may be a reproduction or modernly altered. Caution is the key, and I try to caution in every book I write to take some time and study the traits found on known authentic examples so you can compare those to the traits found on artifacts you are considering adding to your collection.

No one can jump into any hobby and instantly be an expert. It simply takes time and dedication to learn what needs to be learned to reach a comfort level. That comfort level increases the longer you collect, but only if proper time is spent studying. I have known people who have collected for decades who still are not very adept at recognizing fakes. At the same time, I have seen collectors come into the hobby and within a couple of years be very skilled at identifying and avoiding questionable items. It is simply a matter of how much time is dedicated to learning.

While many questionable relics can be avoided based on traits seen with the naked eye, or felt with an educated touch, the use of magnification, to me, is a must. Viewing the surface of an artifact at 10x to 30x magnification will give you a thousand times the information you are looking for to make a determination of real vs. fake. Things such as improper patina, rough hinge fractures, sanding striations, improper grinding, metal traces, fake minerals, sanded edges, and lack of proper weathering are all things that can be learned by studying artifacts under magnification.

While jewelers' loupes and hand magnifiers are helpful, I would strongly encourage any person serious about avoiding reproduction and altered items to invest a few hundred dollars in a 10x – 30x stereoscope with a built-in light. They are readily available on eBay and elsewhere, and in my opinion, truly the best investment any collector can make.

For information on books written by Jim Bennett on the topic of avoiding reproductions, visit his website at www.oldrelics.com.

SHOW AND TELL

What better way to conclude a book on flint artifacts than to show some nice frames of flint relics that I came upon while putting together the pictures for this book.

Frame of Knife River flint artifacts found in North Dakota. Collection of Larry Bumann.

Frame of Knife River flint artifacts found in North Dakota. Collection of Larry Bumann.

SHOW AND TELL

Frame of Knife River flint artifacts found in North Dakota. Collection of Larry Bumann.

Frame of Knife River flint artifacts found in North Dakota. Collection of Larry Bumann.

SHOW AND TELL

Frame of Knife River flint artifacts found in North Dakota. Collection of Larry Bumann.

Frame of Knife River flint artifacts found in North Dakota. Collection of Larry Bumann.

SHOW AND TELL

Frame of Knife River flint artifacts found in North Dakota. Collection of Larry Bumann.

Frame of flint artifacts found between 1985 to 2005 in Fairfield and Knox Co., Ohio. The center Dovetail measures 3½". Collection of Mark Morrison. Personal finds.

Frame of flint artifacts found between 1985 and 2005 in Fairfield and Knox Co., Ohio. The center Stringtown measures 4½". Collection of Mark Morrison. Personal finds.

Beautiful frame of drills from the collection of Ron L. Harris.

Nice frame of flint artifacts from the collection of Ron L. Harris.

Group of hafted scrapers and knives found in North Carolina and north Georgia. Collection of Ron L. Harris. Personal finds.

Group of knives, scrapers, and choppers from the North Carolina Piedmont Region. All were recovered between 1957 and 1973. Collection of Ron L. Harris. Personal finds.

Exceptional frame of Florida artifacts from the collection of Rick Schwardt.

Exceptional frame of Florida artifacts from the collection of Rick Schwardt.

SHOW AND TELL

Beautiful set of Shoshone knives found in various western states. Collection of Gordon Erspamer.

Drills from various counties in North Carolina. Largest is 3¼". Collection of Frank Loverso. Most are personal finds.

Group of drills found in Scioto and Lawrence Co., Ohio. The longest is 2¼". Collection of Steve Valentine. Personal finds.

SHOW AND TELL

The following set of photographs are a great selection of flint relics assembled by one of the hobby's respected collectors. While visiting a show in Pryor, Oklahoma, a couple of years ago I found myself at Chris Merriam's table talking relics and looking over this wonderful frame of flint artifacts he has put together over the years. It was just too nice a selection not to photograph and feature here. Chris is one of those easy-going collectors that once you meet, you always stop by to visit with when you see him out at the shows. Chris also has a nice website at www.arrowheadsonline.com with some great artifacts.

Some of the exceptional artifacts pictured in this frame of relics are:

3⅞" Calf Creek found by Tim Harvell in Tulsa Co., Oklahoma. One ear was broken during notching, made of banded Kay County chert.

4⅛" Neosho found in northeast Oklahoma. Ex. Greg Perino #336.

4½" Angostura knife made of Frisco chert found near Paul's Valley, OK.

Gahagan blade made from Edward's Plateau chert. It is 4¹³⁄₁₆" long, 1³⁄₁₆" wide, an incredible ⅛" thick, and ³⁄₁₆" at it thickest spot, one of the thinnest blades I have seen. Found at the Miller's Crossing site in Arkansas.

5–3¾" base tang made of Trout Creek chert, found by Ted Winters near Fairplay, Colorado.

4¼" Neosho found in Sumner Co., Kansas, and made from Alibates flint.

Mineral Springs blade, 7" long, ¼" thick, made of Edwards Plateau chert.

Caddo blade from Bowie Co., Texas., found by Mike Teehee. It is 6⅝" long and ⁵⁄₁₆" thick, Edwards Plateau.

Bennett's
Ancient Artifacts & Auctions
P.O. Box 315 Polk, OH 44866

Jim Bennett 419-945-2893

Over 12 Auctions Every Year!
All Artifacts GUARANTEED Authentic
Artifacts from Coast-to-Coast In Our Sales
Consign Your Artifacts Today! Low 15% Fee!

Visit Us Online!   www.oldrelics.com

Bennett's
Artifact Authentication
P.O. Box 315 Polk, OH 44866

Jim Bennett   419-945-2893

Jim Bennett is a published author of 7 books on Indian artifacts including several titles devoted specifically to determining artifact authenticity. Jim is now offering authentication services on artifacts from the general Midwest & East coast areas.

If you are looking for an honest opinion you can trust based on 25 years experience studying ancient artifacts, Bennett's is ready to assist you.

For More Information Visit
www.Bennettauthentications.com

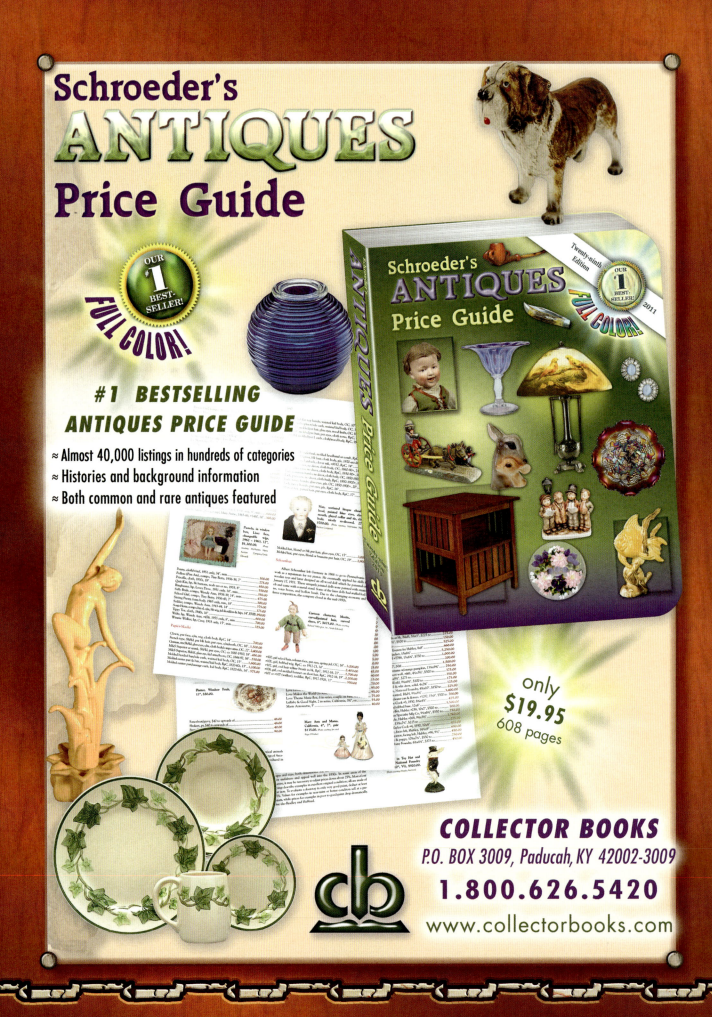